MALABAR AND THE DUTCH

MALABAR AND THE DUTCH

BEING THE HISTORY OF THE FALL OF THE NAYAR POWER IN MALABAR

K. M. PANIKKAR

GYAN

Published by

Gyan Publishing House
5, Ansari Road
Daryaganj, New Delhi-110002
Phone: 011-47034999, 9811692060
E-mail: books@gyanbooks.com

Distribution Network
gyanbooks.com
India, USA, Canada, UK, Australia

ISBN: 978-93-7316-512-7 (PB)

First Published, 1931

2nd Impression 2025

Printed at: Gyan Press, Delhi.

MALABAR AND THE DUTCH
Arthur: K. M. PANIKKAR

MALABAR AND THE DUTCH

TARAPOREVALA
EST. 1864
BOMBAY

"Mr. Panikkar is the author of excellent historical works. He is a thoughtful author and brings much study to bear upon the subjects which he discusses. His works deserve appreciation for scholarship and research."—*The Hindustan Review.*

"He is a writer of the advanced guard of the best Indian Political thought, who writes with the same respect for other participants in the controversies as he would look for from them, and who forms his conclusions without fear or favour, and states them with frankness and courage."—*The Times of India.*

"Mr. Panikkar is well-known as an able and thoughtful writer. He often provokes disagreement, but he is hardly ever unfair; an opponent can always see the reasonableness of his point of view."—*The Times Literary Supplement.* (London)

"In summarising the history Mr. Panikkar gives a scholarly account of the Government and social conditions." *Boston Evening Transcript.*

"His *Malabar and the Portuguese* is the first comprehensive history of the dealings of the Portuguese in the West Coast of India, ably written and interesting." *Sunday Express.* (London)

"He shows considerable skill and analytical acumen." —*The Hindu.*

"He is quite the best writer among Indian publicists. He is candid and his suggestions are therefore always illuminating." — *The Manchester Guardian.*

"He writes from the National standpoint, but he is moderate in tone. He takes a broader view of the situations than writers usually take. We have nothing but praise to offer." — *The Near East and India.* (London)

"He has his own views; but he understands and deals appreciatively with the views of others. He is a master in the art of seeing events as one whole and handles his material with ease." —*The Statesman.*

"He writes with commendable moderation." —*The Daily Telegraph.* (London)

"Written by a deft hand, sure of its facts and not lacking in originality of thought and presentation, his works are very stimulating even to a lay reader. To the historical scholar they are quite an intellectual treat." *Mysore Economic Journal.*

This Dutch Map of Southern India is from the India Office Records Department. It has not been published before. Though the map is undated there is sufficient internal evidence to its date. The Kingdoms of Bijapur and Golkonda which are clearly marked show that the political conditions represented are prior to the annexation of these States. The Marathas are not marked at all. Besides, Cochin is shown as being Portuguese while Quilon is marked without any indication of its political status. In any case, therefore, the map was drawn before 1663; and it is likely that it represents the political divisions in India in 1660.

MALABAR AND THE DUTCH

(Being the History of the Fall of the Nayar Power in Malabar)

BY

K. M. PANIKKAR, B. A. (Oxon.),

Barrister-at-law,

DIXON SCHOLAR OF CHRIST CHURCH, OXFORD

Sometime Professor of Modern History, Muslim University, Aligarh.

Author of "Malabar and the Portuguese", "The relations of Indian States with the Government of India", "Shri Harsha of Kanauj", Etc.

FOREWORD

BY

Sir EVAN COTTON, K. C. I. E.,

Late President of the Bengal Legislative Council, and President of Historical Records Commission, etc.

BOMBAY:

D. B. TARAPOREVALA SONS & CO.

"KITAB MAHAL": HORNBY ROAD

DEDICATED BY PERMISSION

TO

His Highness Sri Maharaja Rama Varma,

G. C. S. I., G. C. I. E.

OF COCHIN

FOREWORD

In his book on "Malabar and the Portuguese", Mr. Panikkar has traced the history of the relations of the Portuguese with the West Coast of India from 1500 to 1663. He has shown that their political organisation was singularly ineffective; that outside Goa which was an easily defensible island their authority never extended beyond a few coastal towns, and that the monopoly of trade which they claimed, was never conceded by the Indian Powers. In the present volume we are presented with a survey of the Dutch connection with Malabar, which may be said to begin with the capture of Cochin from the Portuguese in 1663 and lingered on until the surrender of that place to Major Petrie in 1795, when the Dutch flag ceased to fly on the West Coast. The period is of special interest because it witnessed the fall of the Nayar power—a subject with which Mr. Panikkar, as a member of the Nayar caste, is peculiarly competent to deal.

The Nayars are the most characteristic though not the most numerous of the communities in Malabar. In its widest sense the term includes a very large number of castes which are now quite distinct. But there can be little doubt that the real Nayars were primarily a military caste. They are the feudal and military aristocrats of the West Coast. Burke, in one of his speeches on the French Revolution, classed them with the Mamalukes of Egypt; and they have been famous since the days of Marco Polo. Traces of the martial spirit, which attracted the notice of Gaspar Correa and Duarte Barbosa, and many other early travellers, survive in the *Kalaris*, a sort of combined private chapel and gymnasium, or fencing school, which are still attached to high-class Nayar houses. There is an instructor-in-arms to the family of the Zamorin of Calicut, who is known as the Dharmoth Panikkar, and whose ancestors were the hereditary Commanders-in-Chief. In modern times, however, the Nayars have exchanged the sword for the pen although they still own much land, and have secured a substantial share of the professions and of posts in the Government service in the Madras Presidency. Their origin is obscure. Sir C. Sankaran Nayar, one of the most distinguished members of the caste, has expressed the belief, in conversation with the writer, that they came in the first instance from the North, and has mentioned in support of his view that the dialect spoken at Delhi contains many words which bear a close resemblance to Malayalam. They are certainly not the original aboriginal inhabitants, for there can be no doubt of the large admixture of Aryan blood. Their religious beliefs exhibit a strange combination of Hindu and Dravidian cults. In this connection Mr. Panikkar has observed elsewhere (Journal of the Royal Anthropological Institute, Vol. XLVIII) that after twenty centuries of conflict with Hinduism, the Nayars cling with extreme persistence to spirit worship. But perhaps the most remarkable feature of their social system is the *tarawad*, a family establishment which consists of all the descendants from the same ancestress, counting relationship exclusively from the side of the mother. Property is owned in common and is under the control of the senior male member who is known as the *karnavan*; but the head of the family is the senior lady, and children belong to their mother's *tarawad*.

The Travancore State, which is to-day the principal state on the Malabar Coast and extends over an area of 7625 square miles, was founded on the ruin of the Nayar Power. In 1762 the military hegemony of the Nayars in Travancore and in the adjoining state of Cochin was finally broken. The Zamorin of Calicut, who represents the historic dynasty which was reigning in Malabar when the Portuguese first landed on the Coast, is now merely a wealthy landholder shorn of all sovereign authority. When the great Martanda Varma ascended the throne of Travancore in 1729, his state was one of the smallest in Malabar. When he died in 1758, he had established an autocracy over the West Coast, which Mr. Panikkar describes as the victory of Tamilian over Malayali culture. Nevertheless, his family claims to be, as indeed they are, Malabar Kshattriyas, and the succession is rigidly maintained through the female line. The sons of the Maharajah are of no account; the heir-apparent is the eldest male of the Maharájah's *Tarawad.* It has been said that but for foreign intervention the ascendancy of the Nayars might have endured for centuries to come; and the comment is justified. Mr. Panikkar shows us how their fall was associated with the presence of the Dutch in Malabar. "The United Company of the Netherlands" was a very powerful organism. Professor Greyl, in the chapter on "The Dutch in India" which he contributed to the fifth volume of the *Cambridge History of India,* has given us an admirable account of its composition. It was made up of six "chambers" which traded each with its own capital but pooled their profits and losses. The Amsterdam chamber which was the most important, appointed eight out of the seventeen directors who held office for life. But the "Assembly of the Noble Lords of the Seventeen", which met three times a year, was concerned only with the general lines of policy: the executive authority rested with the several chambers which were situated in the various towns. By the charter of March 20, 1602, the Company was given the exclusive right to trade in all countries between the Cape of Good Hope and the Straits of Magellan; and in 1609 the 1st Governor-General of the Dutch possessions in the East Indies was appointed. Ten years later the famous Jan Pietersoon Coen whose name is perpetuated by one of the steamers of the Nederland Royal Mail line, founded the city of Batavia in the Island of Java on the ruins of Jacatra, and made it his headquarters.

As Mr. Panikkar has pointed out, the first connection of the Dutch with Malabar began as early as 1604, when Admiral Steven van der Haghen concluded a treaty with the Zamorin of Calicut, who was chafing under the constant interference of the Portuguese. But it was not until October 1661 that any definite action was taken. Quilon and Cranganore were captured; and with the fall of Cochin in January 1663, the Dutch stepped into the shoes of the Portuguese. During the next century and a quarter, their policy was governed, as Mr. Panikkar observes, by "a single consideration—that of obtaining the greatest share in the pepper trade at a minimum cost. The *Commandeur*, or head of the administration, whose jurisdiction extended over the Malabar Coast, Kanara and Vengurla, resided at Cochin, where the fortress of Nieuu Oranje had been built in 1662. His rank was not a high one in the Dutch Colonial hierarchy; and it was speedily discovered that the establishment of a monopoly in the pepper trade could not be realised. The expenditure more than outweighed the advantages. They were never (Mr. Panikkar insists) the Paramount power in Malabar. Their political authority was confined to Cochin and its neighbourhood and to Quilon. The rise of Travancore was fatal to their military pretensions and eventually they were engulfed in the growing tide of British dominion. At the same time, they were superior to the Portuguese in many respects. Their officers were competent businessmen: and on the whole they were liberal and tolerant. Their one idea was trade, and Mr. Panikkar is of opinion that their connection with Malabar was in many ways beneficial. The *Hortus Malabaricus*, which was compiled at Cochin from 1678 onwards under the patronage of Baron Hendrik Adriaan van Rheede of Drakenstegn—some say by a Carmelite friar named Matthacus, others by Johannes Casearius, a Protestant pastor—testifies to their zeal for scientific research. Similarly, Philippus Baldaeus' description of Ceylon and the Malabar Coast, which was published at Amsterdam in 1672, and of which there is an English translation in the third volume of Churchill's *Voyages* (1745), was the work of another minister of the Dutch Reformed Church.

Among the remarkable men in the service of the Dutch East India Company, van Rheede takes a high place. He was commandeur at Cochin from 1673 to 1677; and his tomb in the Dutch Cemetery at Surat, where he died on December 15, 1691, is one of the sights of the town. He was appointed by the Seventeen in 1684 as "Commissar General for the Western Quarters", and held the office until his death. The mausoleum, which is said to have been built with the intention of eclipsing that of Sir George Oxinden, consists of a double cupola of great dimensions with a gallery above and below, supported on handsome columns. The curious will notice that in the inscription, "Cochin" and "Souratte" are engraved in capital letters and "bombai" in small ones. It was during Van Rheede's administration of Malabar that the Cochin State was virtually handed over to the Dutch.

Of a very different type, but no less remarkable, was the Valia Kappithan or "Great Captain", Eustache Benedict de Lannoy. He was a Flemming and was originally in the Dutch service, but was taken prisoner by Martanda Varma, with twenty-three other Europeans, at the battle of Colachel on August 10, 1741, which put an end to the Dutch dreams of the conquest of Malabar. Together with another prisoner, a Frenchman of the name of Doncaud, he entered the service of the Maharajah and organised his army for him. The famous Travancore lines which were taken by Tippu in 1790 were built by him, and also the fort of Udayagiri, the walls of which enclose a hill, thirty-eight miles to the south-east of Trivandrum. He died in June 1777 at the age of sixty-two and is buried at Udayagiri. Like Monsieur Raymond at Hyderabad, who has given his name to the Myseram Risala in the Nizam's Army, he is still remembered as "Istach".

What memorials have the Dutch left behind them in Southern India? Most of them are on the Coromandel Coast—ornamented tombs at Negapatam, Pulicat (Castel Geldria) and Sadras, Porto Novo, Bimlipatam and Masulipatam (Bunder). In the extreme south, at Cape Comorin are the ruins of Dutch fortifications and a huge granite slab, nine feet in height, now used as a doorstep, originally erected in memory of a Dutch factor. Hard by, at Tuticorin, is a well-filled Dutch burying ground. On the West Coast, there are the regal mausoleums at Surat. In Malabar itself we shall find at Cannanore on the outer ramparts of Fort St. Angelo, the grave of the wife and two children (1745) of Godfried Weyerman, who was Governor of Cochin from 1761 to 1764. At Tangacherry (Tangasseri), a minute British possession of 96 acres in extent, situated on the coast two miles from Quilon, is the grave (1779) of a Dutch Commandant of

Fort Thomas, which was originally built by the Portuguese in 1503, and has almost entirely fallen into the sea. There is rather more at Cochin itself. The modern Town of Cochin, or Kuchi Bunder, is in British territory. It is a busy little port, picturesquely situated on the northern end of a long sandy spit lying between the backwater and the sea at the mouth of the Cochin river. Three miles across the lagoon at the southern end is Muttancheri, which is in Cochin state territory, and is famous for its two synagogues of the White and Black Jews. On the island of Bolghotty, in the lagoon, is the British Residency, which was built by the Dutch in 1744. The Dutch tombstones in the church of St. Francis which are ranged against the walls with their Portuguese predecessors, date from 1664: among them are those which once covered the last resting-place of Doctor Balthasar de Meter (1666) who, according to Governor Adrian Moens, was the first Protestant Minister to preach in Cochin, Abraham Cornelis de la Haye (1752) who was governor from 1750 to 1751, the wife and daughter (1688) of Isaac van Dielen, Governor from 1687 to 1693, the wife (1727) of Jacob de Jong, Governor from 1724 to 1731, and the children (1739) of van Gollenesse, Governor from 1735 to 1743. The church, which was originally built by the Franciscans and is believed to be the oldest in India, was converted by the Dutch into a Protestant place of worship. The old Portuguese cathedral of Santa Cruz has vanished; it was formed into a warehouse by the Dutch and was blown up for strategic reasons in 1806 by the British together with the fort and some of the quays and houses. The military commandant's house can still be seen, but two gates, close to the English Club, mark all that is left of the governor's residence. In the Dutch Cemetery is the grave (1784) of the wife of Jan Lambertus Vanspall, the last governor, who surrendered to the British on October 20, 1795, after the firing of a single shell "planted with excellent skill in the centre of Government House." There were until recently—and probably still are—Vanspalls on the west coast, and Mr. J. J. Cotton, in his *List of Monumental Inscriptions in the Madras Presidency* (p. 261) relates that there is a tradition among them that a great fortune awaits the Vanspall who has the ability to prove to the Netherlands government that he is descended from the governor of Cochin.

The visitor to India rarely finds his way to Malabar. He misses much. The scenery is delightful: the castes and customs amply repay study; and Malabar is one of the few places in the world where the accuracy of observations made four centuries ago can be checked on the spot. It is to be hoped that Mr. Panikkar's historical researches will tempt many to cultivate acquaintance with his subject at first hand. He is one of that rapidly growing body of Indian scholars who have enriched the history of their country by illustrations from original vernacular documents. Of these there are many in Malabar in the temples and in the custody of the principal families: and Mr. Panikkar has been fortunate enough to obtain access to them. It is in this respect that his work is especially valuable: for these papers frequently throw an entirely new light upon controversies and episodes which are apt to be coloured by their presentation by foreign observers.

EVAN COTTON

CONTENTS

INTRODUCTION

This book is a sequel to my earlier volume on Malabar and the Portuguese. The study of the relations of the Portuguese with the West coast of India has a special interest to the general reader as the Portuguese were the first power to trade direct with India. Though the Dutch connection with Malabar has no such wider appeal, yet, from another point of view, the period is one of special interest to the students of history. From the point of view of administrative organisation the Dutch East India Company was the accepted model of its more celebrated rival, the English East India Company. To the student of the economic history of the 17th and the 18th centuries the relations of Malabar with Europe cannot also fail to be of interest.

So far as the history of Malabar is concerned this period is all-important. It witnessed the downfall of the Nayar hegemony and the rise of the modern political systems. The division of Kerala into Travancore, Cochin and British Malabar is the outcome of the political events of this period. The disappearance of the powerful baronage who had so long maintained their hold against monarchical authority, the development of internal and external trade and the establishment of ordered forms of government are among the other features of this period.

Ample material for the study of the period is available in Dutch, English and Malayalam. In the case of the early Portuguese period the students of history have to depend almost entirely on Portuguese sources; but fortunately for the 17th and 18th century the presence of the English on the West Coast enables us to check the Dutch records from English sources.

The Records that the Dutch left with regard to the administration of their factories in Malabar are in many ways unique. Each commandeur left for his successor a *memoir* dealing with the affairs of the Company and in general with the condition of

Malabar. This series, of which the following have been published, constitute a mine of information about Malabar.

Memoir of	J. V. S. Van Gollenesse	1908
,,	Adriaan V. Moens	1908
,,	Commandeur F. Cunes	1908
,,	J. G. Angelbeak	1908
,,	C. Breakpot	1909
,,	De Jong	1909
,,	G. Weijermann	1910
,,	Van Rheede	1911

The *memoir* of Moens, which is the most important of these, is an elaborate document, giving a descriptive account of the conditions in Malabar. The supreme government at Batavia had asked him to submit to them all available information together with a map of Malabar if procurable; and Moens therefore wrote not merely for the information of his successor but for the benefit of his superiors. The memoirs of Moens and Gollenesse have been translated and published under the title of *The Dutch in Malabar.*

The India Office in London possesses a large number of transcripts from Dutch Records at the Hague. Thirty-six volumes are available in translation and these are indeed very valuable. But the main collection of Records relating to Cochin is in the Record Office, Madras. An analytical list of these records has been published by the Madras Government under the title of "*A Press list of Ancient Dutch Records from 1657 to 1825.*"

At the Hague at the Rijkarchief there is a very great deal of material available. Owing to the shortness of my stay in Holland I was not able to make full use of these.

The following published works deal with the Dutch affairs in relation to the mainland of India.

Aalbers, J. Rijeklof Van Goens.

Imhoff Van. Considerations sun letat present de la compagnie hollandaise des Indes orientales. Hague 1741.

Stellwagen: Gustaf Wilhelm Baron Van Imhoff (de Indische Gids) 1889.

Veth. Adriaan Van Rheede De indische gids 1887. Vol. III and IV.

Philip Baldeus. Description of Malabar and Coromandel. Churchill's Voyages Vol. III, 1748.

Day, Francis. The Land of the Perumals.

C. Atchuta Menon. The Cochin State Manual.

Vischer. Letters from Malabar.

Menon. History of Kerala. Ernakulam 1924.

Menon. History of Cochin 2 Vols. (in Malayalam).

Nagam Aiyya. Travancore State Manual (3 Vols.).

J. J. Cotton. European Monuments in Madras.

There is a very considerable amount of material available in Malayalam. The *granthavaries* or chronicles of Trippunithura, Cochin, and the Records at Paliyam are becoming gradually available to the public. So far, the private records in important families have been treated as something mysterious and students have had no access to them. The Travancore archaeological department has however published important plates belonging to the Paliyam family. Owing to the efforts of P. Anujan Achan of Paliyam some of the more important records of the leading families in Cochin are now being published. The Cochin archaeological department has also published some of the important Malayalam letters addressed by the Rajah to the Supreme Council at Batavia. It would be a very great service to the history of Malabar if at least a Catalogue of the private collections is made by the archaeological departments of these States and published for the information of students.

Among the published Malayalam books belonging to this period which have been of use there are two which deserve special mention. They are the *Patappattu* or the "Ballad of War" and the *Mamankodharanam*. The *Patappattu*, which deals with the war of Cochin succession leading to the expulsion of the Portuguese, is a historical narrative of great value. Its facts and chronology are exceptionally accurate. Though devoid of any great literary merit, as a historical composition it takes a high rank in Malayalam, especially for its non-partisan spirit. The book has been edited with an excellent introduction for the Government of Travancore by Mr. Oolloor Parameswara Aiyyar, a renowned poet and scholar of Malabar. The *Mamankodharanam*, unlike *Patappattu*, does not claim to be non-partisan. It is written frankly in praise of the great Zamorin who helped the Dutch and the Rajah of Cochin in the war of Vettom succession. It deals with the history of that period from the point of view of a courtier of the Calicut Ruler. This book has been edited with a learned introduction and valuable notes by K. C. Mana Vikraman Raja of the Zamorin's family.

It only remains for me to acknowledge my obligations. I am grateful to Sir Evan Cotton, who was kind enough to read through the manuscript and to contribute a learned and valuable introduction. His deep interest in Indian History needs no acknowledgment from me. I am also obliged to him for procuring me from the Records of the India Office an excellent contemporary map of South India. I must also express my obligations to Mlle Irene Marcousse who helped me with the Dutch Records at the India Office.

K. M. Panikkar

MALABAR AND THE DUTCH

CHAPTER I

THE ARRIVAL OF THE DUTCH IN MALABAR

The Dutch had for long looked on with jealousy at the monopoly which the Portuguese enjoyed in the trade of the East. But the colossal power of Philip II of Spain who had also become the king of Portugal made any direct challenge to his naval power impossible for a long time. It was only after the defeat of the Spanish Armada and the consequent blow to the naval prestige of Spain that the Dutch were emboldened to challenge the Portuguese in the Indian Seas. In 1592 at a meeting of the leading Dutch merchants held at Amsterdam it was decided to found a company for trading with India. In order to secure the necessary information about the route and to gather a general idea of the conditions of the voyage Cornelius de Houtman was sent to Lisbon. The Company also had in their possession a map of the Indian sea prepared by Pitrus Plaucius, the Geographer. But the most important information available to them came from the traveller Linchoten. Jan Huyghen Linchoten went out to India as secretary to the Archbishop of Goa. Linchoten was a careful observer and a penetrating student of affairs. On his return he was a very enthusiastic promoter of the Dutch enterprise and his advice and information were earnestly sought by the Dutch merchants. In 1595 a fleet of four vessels commanded by Cornelius de Houtman was fitted out and sent to the East. The arrival of the Dutch on Indian waters changed the whole political situation in Malabar. The Princes on the coast saw that the Portuguese who had so far held supremacy on the sea were on the defensive against the intruders whose power they could not resist. The first connection of the Dutch with the Malabar was the treaty they negotiated with the Zamorin as early as 1604. By this treaty which was concluded between "the Zamorin, Emperor of Malabar and Admiral S. Van der Hagen...... with a view to the expulsion of the Portuguese from the territories of His Highness and the rest of India" the Dutch were allowed to trade at Calicut and to build a fort for their protection.[1]

Before the Dutch evolved any regular policy with regard to Malabar, they secured an effective footing in Java and the Eastern Archipelago and the next half a century was devoted to the development of their authority in these areas and to the control of the Eastern seas. The Malabar coast, however, was not wholly forgotten. In 1642 the Dutch negotiated a treaty with "Siam Batshery vambar" the Rajah of Procaud.[2] They also visited and kept up friendly relations with other coastal rulers.

---

1) India Office Records.
Dutch Treaties etc., Vol. I. Page 131.

2) Nieuhoff, p. 224.

But it was only after the capture of Colombo and their firm establishment in Ceylon that they were able to turn their attention to the Malabar coast. With a base in Ceylon it was possible for them to take effective action against the Portuguese. Events in Malabar favoured them. The Portuguese had forcibly interfered in the affairs of Cochin. A war of succession had broken out in that state as a series of conflicting adoptions gave rise to rival claims to the throne.[1] As a result of this, the elder branch was expelled by the claimants of the junior branch with the help of the Portuguese. In 1658 when the ruling Rajah died another adoption was made from Tanur, a principality which had been traditionally friendly to the Portuguese. By this act, the elder branch was again excluded from succession.

The dispossessed prince of the elder branch was advised by the Paliyam chief, the premier nobleman of Cochin, to visit Colombo and negotiate with the Dutch Company. That prince, though in bad health, did not hesitate to undertake what was then an arduous voyage and he was able to persuade the Dutch Company to undertake the expulsion of the Portuguese from Cochin. The Dutch commander well knew that this was the golden opportunity for him. The cause of the dispossessed branch had strong and ardent supporters in Malabar. The Zamorin was on their side. The Rajahs of Vadakumkur and Thekkumkur were also their supporters. More, the hereditary prime minister

1) For a detailed account of these troubles the reader is referred to the author's Malabar and the Portuguese. Page 155 et seq.

of Cochin, the Chief of Paliyam, was also secretly in league with them. An expedition had therefore every chance of success. The Dutch had been long maturing their plans for the expulsion of the Portuguese from the Malabar seas. The invitation of the dispossessed prince of Cochin afforded them a suitable opportunity. De Weert had very early foreseen that the Portuguese naval power in India was doomed once it had ceased to exist in Cochin. "When they (the Portuguese) are once turned out of Cochin they are out of India", he had declared. In 1658 when their plans were maturing Van Goens wrote as follows to the Governor-General and Council of India:[1] "We expect they will have received reinforcements by next year for which we must also be prepared in order to maintain our supremacy on the sea. It is a pity that our fleet generally reaches Goa too late. We should therefore propose that the next expedition leave Batavia about September 15th and sail direct for Ceylon, where it could be strengthened with some small craft carrying a crew of no more than 15 men which we have found very useful against the frigates in our last exploit.

"With these combined forces we could then make an attempt on Cochin where the Portuguese could collect their strongest naval forces and if we are so lucky as to defeat them the whole coast of Malabar and the pepper trade will be ours. We could have at Cochin a redoubt of 100 men and give the town in charge of the Zamorin on condition to sell us the pepper at a fixed price." He

1) Letter dated March 17th, 1658.

recommended that Roothers should be appointed commander of the fleet.

On July 6th, 1658 Van Goens again wrote to Jan Matsuycker who was then the Governor-General that the Portuguese had collected 40 frigates at Cochin and that the movements of the Dutch were being watched. He stated that they could muster about 700 European soldiers in Ceylon and if another 600 could be sent from Batavia he was confident of success. His idea was to go first to Cochin. "The town, when the fleet was destroyed, could not offer much resistance."

By the end of 1658 it was clear to the Portuguese that the Dutch were bent on forcing the issue with them on the Indian seas. The Governors of India, Francis de Mello de Castro and Antonio de Sousa Coutinho jointly addressed the king of Portugal an important communication[1] in which they explained the position of affairs with the utmost frankness. They stated: "we feel it our bounden duty to acquaint you with the position of affairs in India and to inform you that unless we are properly assisted the whole of your Majesty's possessions (in India) will be lost." They pointed out that they had no money in the treasury and that as for the equipment of the fleet they had to borrow from private individuals. "We earnestly implore your majesty to send us by next year adequate reinforcements, otherwise we shall not be able to resist the enemy at all."

After the letter was written but before it was des-

1) Letter dated 18th Dec., 1658. See Malabar and the Portuguese p. 157 et seq.

patched the governors received the news that Quilon had fallen and that the Dutch fleet was off Cochin.

Fortunately for the Portuguese the schemes of Van Goens could not be carried out in 1659, as he had hoped, because he had to send the troops he had collected to Amboina. The fight between the Portuguese and the Dutch and the conquest of Cochin by the latter have been described by me elsewhere.[1] It is unnecessary to repeat it here as it deals more with the Portuguese period and the reader is referred to Chapter X of "Malabar and the Portuguese".

As soon as the Portuguese were expelled from Cochin, Van Goens established himself in the fort and took in hand the consolidation of the commercial and political power of the Company on the Malabar Coast.

The position of the Dutch in 1603 differed materially from that of the Portuguese at the time of da Gama and Almeida. The Portuguese had to build up political and commercial relations with the Malabar chiefs who were suspicious of the newcomers and often openly hostile to them. Besides, they had also to face the power of the Mohammedan trading community who enjoyed a monopoly of commerce on the west coast. The Dutch on the other hand saw a commercial and political system already established and by their conquest of Cochin they stepped into the shoes of the Portuguese. They claimed all the rights which the Portuguese enjoyed in Cochin and treated the Rajah of the place as Martim de Sousa and other

1) See Malabar and the Portuguese. op. cit.

Portuguese viceroys had treated him. All over Malabar the Dutch took over the Portuguese system and administered it with superior efficiency and with a larger attention to profits. In a later chapter we shall discuss at some length the organisation and methods of the Dutch Company as compared to the system which the Portuguese developed.

The Dutch were also at an advantage in that the commercial power of the great Moorish houses on the coast had been completely shattered in the previous century. They found themselves therefore left without serious competition in the internal trade of the country. The Moorish trading community was practically non-existent in Cochin and in its stead there had grown up the "Canarenes", a Hindu Community from the Konkan districts who worked as the agents of the Portuguese. The "Canarenes"—or as we now call them the Konkanis—were wholly dependent on their European masters, so that when the Portuguese went away from Cochin they became equally serviceable to the Dutch.

In one thing however the position of the Dutch was not so advantageous as that of the Portuguese. From the earliest days of the Dutch connection with Malabar, there was looming in the background the competition of more powerful European nations—the French and the English. The English were already established at Tellichery and in 1664 the Rajah of Purakkad invited them to establish themselves there. Further south the English had also a factory at Anjengo where they established themselves under the protection of the Rani of Attungal. The French did not come immediately into the field but from their base in the Ile de France it was easy for them at any time to establish themselves on the Malabar Coast.

The most important fact was, however, that the Dutch inherited from the Portuguese a system of political relations with the Rajahs and Kings of the Malabar Coast which gave them definite rights on which to build. The Cochin Rajah was accepted from the beginning as a vassal whose rights were derived from the Company. The very fact that they had placed him on the *Gadi* and his authority was dependent on their support made them look upon him as a Ruler in whose affairs they had a right to intervene. The Chief of Paliyam who was the Minister of Cochin had already been taken under their protection and was the company's liegeman.[1] He had pledged his state, his subjects and his person to the Company. With the rulers and chiefs in the immediate neighbourhood of Cochin, like Mangat and Parur, and with the feudatories of the Cochin Rajah the Dutch claimed all the rights of a suzerain and overlord. With the Zamorin their relations were even older. We have noticed the treaty between Van der Hagen and that Ruler in 1604.[2] Before the attack on Cochin in 1662 Admiral Van Goens signed a new treaty with the Zamorin by which the Dutch secured the right to the exclusive purchase of pepper in Calicut territory at the market price and the Zamorin was promised in exchange the

1) India Office Records. Dutch Records Vol. II.
2) Treaties etc. Vol. I. page 131.

Island of Vaipeen. As soon as the campaign was over the Zamorin demanded that the position of the Cochin Rajah should be reduced to what it was before the Portuguese elevated him to the status of an independent ruler and that Vaipeen should be annexed to Calicut territories. Van Goens rejected both of these demands with the result that the relations between the Zamorin and the Dutch were no better than those which subsisted between him and the Portuguese. The most important campaigns that the Dutch had to undertake, which financially ruined the Company in Malabar, were against the power of Calicut which continued to be a standing menace to the Dutch till the invasion of Malabar by Hyder Ali.

A treaty had also been concluded with the Rajah of Travancore in 1662 at Kallada. The following were the main clauses of the agreement.

Perpetual peace was established between Travancore and the Dutch Company. The native Christians were continued in the same position as under the Portuguese. The Rajah undertook to give a monopoly of pepper trade to the Company and to accept passes from the Dutch Commandeur for all vessels. The admiral undertook in exchange of these concessions to make annual presents to the Rajah of several guns and 15,000 fanams.

It was the trade in pepper that interested the Dutch most and in this they tried to establish a complete monopoly. Even before they had driven out the Portuguese, the Dutch had made arrangements about the transport of the pepper bought in Malabar.

Writing in 1658,[1] Van Goens reported that instructions have already been issued to the envoy to the Naick of Madura that pepper from the Malabar Coast shall only be carried across the Bay by the Company's servants. "This condition must be insisted on and in the event of Cotcheri falling into our hands it will secure the monopoly of pepper trade to us for in the north of Cotcheri pepper is much dearer than Cannanore."

As the establishment of a complete monopoly was possible only by new and more comprehensive agreements with the Malabar Princes, the Company sent out Captain Nieuhoff who was the Factor at Quilon to negotiate with the rulers on the coast. His general instructions, from Jacob Hutstaart, were to secure from the Princes a monopoly for the trade in pepper and in opium.

The first chief whom Nieuhoff visited was the Rajah of Kayamkulam who received him with great courtesy and entered into an agreement on the lines suggested by the Dutch. From Kayamkulam Nieuhoff went to Purakkad but the Rajah was away at Kodamaloor which was the original seat of the family. Nieuhoff followed him there, travelling by boat along the canals of Kuttanad, which he compared in his book to his own native land. The Rajah received him with great cordiality and reminded him how as early as 1640 his family had entered into trade agreements with the Dutch. Nieuhoff mentions[2] that in 1640 the kingdom

1) Van Goens to the Governor-General dated July 6th, 1658.
2) Voyages p. 224.

of Purakkad was ruled by a young prince whom he calls Siam Bateserry Vanbar. He was an ambitious and enterprising ruler and could not brook the interference of the Portuguese against whom he fought successfully for three years. It was during his reign that the Dutch first began to take an effective interest in Malabar. The Rajah made a treaty with the Dutch captain in 1642 by which the East India Company was given the right of trade. The amicable relations did not however continue long as the Rajah of Purakkad supported the Portuguese at Cochin when Van Goens first attacked it. In fact it was the intervention of the Rajah that forced the Dutch to raise the siege. Now that the Dutch were firmly established at Cochin, it was in the interests of the Rajah to forget the recent past and renew the friendly relations that existed before. Nieuhoff describes the Rajah as being "a person of about 30 years of age, very stately and well made". He accepted the suggestion of the Dutch that he should sell all his pepper to them, though he had already given permission to the English to establish a factory at his capital. But when it was further suggested that his pepper should be weighed at Cochin the Rajah objected strongly, stating that it was never the custom at Purakkad to sell through Cochin. Nieuhoff thought it prudent to yield on this issue and an agreement was signed giving the Dutch the monopoly of pepper.

Nieuhoff next visited Madathumkur the petty principality lying between Quilon and Kayamkulam. Though small in extent, Madathumkur was an important centre of pepper trade and Nieuhoff was anxious that the Mohammedans who were settled there should not break the monopoly which the Dutch sought to establish. The envoy took with him the following letter of Jacob Hutstaart to the Rajah.

"ILLUSTRIOUS PRINCE,

"Nothing could be more welcome to me, than to understand at my first arrival in these parts that your Majesty had always been in a good correspondency with our company. To show your Majesty what an extraordinary value we set upon your friendship, we have sent John Nieuhoff, captain of Kailong, in order to enter with you a more strict league and friendship. We hope your Majesty will give him entire credit in what he shall propose to you which I shall be ready to acknowledge on the like occasions.

God preserve and give your Majesty a long and happy life."[1]

After presenting his credentials Nieuhoff broached the question of the trade agreement which found opposition from the considerable Mohammedan community in the state. The Rajah therefore requested Nieuhoff to set down in writing his proposals. The Dutch agent submitted a treaty by which the Rajah was to undertake to forbid the importation of amfion (opium), the peeling of wild cinnamon and the exportation of pepper. The Rajah declined to treat on this footing and seeing him obdurate the Dutch modified their terms and agreed to buy all the pepper produced in

---

1) Letter dated 2nd Feb. 1664. Nieuhoff's Voyages, p. 224.

the land and to withdraw the demand about the peeling of cinnamon.

After settling these contracts Nieuhoff returned to Quilon to interview the King of Travancore. The Rajahs of Travancore claimed to be the head of the five families which between them ruled the territory between Quilon and Cape Comorin. On the 14th of February Nieuhoff went to Attungal to interview the Rajah who received him with courtesy but made him understand through his ministers that he was dissatisfied with the conduct of the Company in burning the palace of the Queen of Quilon. He made it clear that the trade negotiations which Nieuhoff was anxious to take up must include the question of reparations to the Queen of Quilon. While conversations were going on a messenger arrived from the Queen to inform him that the Dutch had not paid the customs due to her nor returned the cannon as they had promised. The minister of Travancore, on hearing this, asked Nieuhoff whether they would do less than the Portuguese had done. The answer was "If we should follow the footsteps of the Portuguese we must be guilty likewise of the same enormities in murthering, plundering, etc., things not customary among us, the intention of the Company being to maintain everyone in his right and to establish a free commerce without interruption".[1] The King of Travancore however refused to proceed further but declared that he would send his minister to Quilon to treat with Nieuhoff. When the captain returned to

1) Nieuhoff p. 226 and 227.

Quilon he found the agent of the Rajah, a general, by name Martanda Pillai, waiting for him. A meeting was arranged at the church of St. Thomas and the following agreement was reached:—

"Nobody shall import, sell or exchange, any amfion into these countries except the Dutch East India Company.

Nobody without exception shall be permitted to export any pepper or cinnamon out of this country or to sell them to anybody except the said company.

A certain price was settled betwixt both parties also; what share each should have in the customs whereby all former pretensions and exceptions should be annulled."

As the questions with regard to the Queen of Quilon were left outstanding, Nieuhoff sent a Topas by name Nicolas de Coasta to her. She refused to yield and demanded that what is hers must be paid first. As this matter was reaching a crisis Jacob Hutstaart himself came down from Cochin. Before his arrival Nieuhoff received a reply from the Queen in the following words:—

"I received and saw the contents of the letter sent to me from John Nieuhoff, Captain of Koilang, concerning the proposed treaty. I will send word in the month of March to Kottekkary where we will meet together and I shall be ready to ratify what my plenipotentiaries shall agree to. For which I ordered this letter to be written to Captain John Nieuhoff."[1]

On the 2nd of March 1664, the representative of the

1) Voyages p. 230.

King of Travancore, whom Nieuhoff calls Kurup, and the Commander Martanda Pillai arrived to accompany him to the Court. The queen received them immediately on arrival in full Durbar surrounded by the officials and nobles. Nieuhoff describes her as being "past middle age, of a brown complexion with black hair knotted in a knot behind, but of a majestic mien, she being a princess who showed a great deal of good conduct in the management of her affairs." A treaty was signed and the queen to show her appreciation of Nieuhoff's efforts to promote good relations between her state and the Company invested him with the Veera Sringala.[1]

After concluding these treaties the Dutch settled down to trade. They soon discovered that as they had no intention to pursue the Portuguese policy of general warfare on the coast beyond the enforcement of their monopoly in spices, the military establishments which they had taken over were a great encumbrance. Hence orders were issued to bring all the fortresses on the coast to a narrower compass.

In 1665 Nieuhoff received orders to draw the city of Quilon within smaller limits and fortify it on the land-side with one or two demi-bastions. He proceeded immediately to demolish "all the houses, churches and trees and what else stood in the way". The foundation of the new fort was laid on the first of July 1665.[2] The same policy was followed in Cochin, though not

1) Veera Sringala is the highest "order" given by Malabar Rulers. It means literally the Bangle of Heroism.

2) Nieuhoff, Page 263.

immediately. The garrison was reduced to one half at Cannanore. At Cranganore also similar reforms were effected. In fact from the very beginning, the Dutch never forgot that their main business was to trade and not to exercise political authority; and with the business of trading they occupied themselves without any loss of time.

CHAPTER II

THE PLIGHT OF THE COCHIN RAJAH

The success or failure of this policy of detailed agreements with the minor princes on the coast for a monopoly in the trade in Malabar spices depended entirely on the Company's ability to control the Rajah of Cochin and to use his position in support of their claims. The total subordination of Cochin was essential if the internal trade which flowed into that port was to be controlled by the factory established on the little island by the shore. Van Goens, therefore, set himself to consolidate his position in Cochin. The pretender to the Cochin throne whose cause the Dutch had supported died before he could be crowned; but his nephew Veera Kerala Varma was placed on the throne. The very ceremony declared the altered position of the Cochin Ruler. The crown bore the arms of the Dutch East India Company, and Van Goens himself, seated on a throne, placed it on the head of the prince. A new treaty with Cochin was signed by which the Dutch were confirmed in the possession of the areas previously in the occupation of the Portuguese, and the Cochin Rajah expressly accepted the protection of the Dutch and placed his state under them. He also guaranteed them a monopoly of pepper and cinnamon and undertook to prohibit the entry of opium into Cochin. The Dutch

Company also received the right of constructing a fort at Cheppuram, another near Alleppy and a third one at the Cochin Harbour. Justice, so far as coastal Christians and half-castes were concerned, was to be divided as it was during the time of the Portuguese.

As the Rajah of Procaud had supported the Portuguese with vigour in the first attack on Cochin and as it was mainly due to his timely naval action that the invaders had to retire, the Dutch were naturally angry with him. A small force was moved against him but no battle took place. On the other hand as the Patappattu says

> "they met as if they were old friends and as if there was never any quarrel between them. And an alliance was formed as of old with the Portuguese."[1]

Following Van Goens, Jacob Hutstaart was for a short time the chief of the Cochin establishment, but he did not remain long. The first commandeur who took up the Cochin post was Ludolf Colster. During his time attention was mostly devoted to the establishment of relations with the other states such as Purakkad, Mangat, Quilon and Vadakkumkur and to the development of the newly secured trade. For the time the Dutch showed no aggressive intentions except with regard to the English factors at Purakkad. Even before the Dutch reached Purakkad, the Rajah of that place, Deva Narayanan, had invited the English to establish a factory at his Capital.[2] In 1665 they estab-

---

1) Patappattu—Srimulam Malayalam Series, Trivandrum. p. 46.
2) British factories in India. 1665—1667. Oxford 1925, p. 90.

lished a small factory there, not so much for trade as for maintaining a footing in the area. Two factors by name Grigby and Harrison were sent down and their instructions were "Should the factors be forced to leave, they must draw up a protest against the Dutch charging them with a great sum annually."[1] According to Grigby the Dutch had in 1665 between Cochin and Quilon 6 watch houses. Taking advantage of a quarrel between a small Dutch landing party and some moors at a place, a few miles south of Purakkad, the commandeur of Cochin came down and established another watch house. When war broke out between England and Holland, the English factory with its guns and ammunition was captured by the Dutch.

Till Hendrick Van Rheede came to Cochin as commandeur in 1673 no definite policy was adopted by the Company towards the Rajahs. Van Rheede was a young officer of noble stock who had distinguished himself at the siege of Cochin. Goens was so highly impressed with his ability and resourcefulness that he recommended him for the post of commandeur at Cochin. As soon as he arrived in Cochin, Van Rheede made it clear that the Dutch Company was not satisfied with the trade of Malabar but desired effective political power. He forced the Rajah of Cochin to make a family settlement which curtailed the authority of the ruler and made him entirely dependent on the Company. The Civil List of the Rajah was settled at 3,000 fanams, of the Elaya Rajah (heir apparent) at 1,500 fanams, and of the

1) British factories in India, p. 90.

other princes in proportion. The junior princes were to take no part in the administration which was handed over to the management of the Paliyam chiefs. This settlement also laid down clearly that no adoption to the Cochin Royal family was to be made without the consent of the Dutch commandeur. A treaty was also made between the Dutch and Eroma (Eravi Varma), the second prince, and Godarma (Godavarma) the fourth prince, on February 23rd 1674 by which the princes promised "that no chiefs will hereafter be elected kings of Cochin but such as are the descendants of the five lawful families of which three are extinct and only two are existing". Not content with this, Van Rheede, on 3rd December 1774, negotiated a treaty with the principal nobles of Cochin i. e. "the thirty thousand Nayars of Karappuram, the three hundred of Badathala, the three hundred of Kandamthurithy, the Meloor Madathil Kymal, the three hundred of Bappeen and those of Paliyattu" by which the contracting parties agreed "for the happiness of the Kingdom of Cochin in general and for their individual welfare respectively to form a league against all those who are the enemies of the Company and of the kingdom of Cochin."

This settlement was naturally much disliked by the princes who rose in revolt against its provisions. The main body of Cochin nobles who resented the intervention of the Dutch in these matters sided with the princes. Civil war broke out and the Rajah himself left his palace and retired to the interior. The Dutch authorities were doubtful of their position especially as the Rajah had withdrawn to the interior and a letter from the Governor-General at Batavia dated 8th September, 1677 was received expostulating with him and requesting him not to stay away but return to the protection and safety of Cochin. The commandeur was not disheartened by these developments. On the other hand, he utilised the weakness of the Rajah to get him to sign another agreement dated 21st May, 1678.[1] This provided that the Company will be allowed to exercise authority without the intervention of the princes—the junior members of the family, that all persons without exception who oppose the Company will be punished, that the princes will not enter the town without the permission of the Rajah, that the Chief of Paliyam will do the needful *in communication* with the Rajah for the welfare of the State and that all the actions and resolutions of the Rajah and his minister will be subject to the approval of the Commandant of Cochin.

This agreement virtually handed over the Cochin state to the Dutch. The Paliyam Chief who was the Company's bondsman was to rule the state, in communication with (not under the orders of) the Rajah. The princes were strictly excluded from all influence. The Rajah himself was reduced to a cypher. Besides all these there was a curious clause which stipulated that the Nayar nobility should not be exempt from punishment.

The earlier agreements had been strongly opposed by the Nayar Chiefs and they had sided with the princes

1) Dutch Records, Treaties Vol. I. p. 386.

in attempting to get the agreements repudiated by the Rajah. This new treaty further enraged the nobles against the Dutch and they openly took up arms with a view to depose the ruler. Matters went so far that the Dutch Company found that if the Rajah whom they had placed on the throne was to be maintained as a pillar of their system, the only method left to them was to interfere openly and take over the management of affairs. The Rajah's officials who were inimical to the Company were also creating trouble with regard to the customs duties at the port. With a view to end all the trouble Martin Huysman, who was the commandeur of Cochin at the time, entered into a new agreement with the Rajah on the 3rd May, 1681. The Rajah was asked to accept a Dutch official as his minister and one of the Canarese subordinates of the Company as his treasurer. The Chief of Paliyam was to be the Prime Minister, but the affairs of the State were to be regulated according to the advice given by the Company's official. The commandeur was only waiting for an opportunity to take over the complete management of the Cochin State and such an opportunity soon occurred. The Chief of Paliyam died leaving a minor as heir to the estate. The vacancy to the prime ministership which thus arose was utilised for the nomination of Captain Hendrik Reins to that post to be held in the name of the minor Chief of Paliyam.

With both the treasury and the dewanship in the hands of the Dutch and with the Paliyam Chief a minor, Cochin becomes less a dependency than a mere proprietary estate of the Dutch Company. The Rajah became a nonentity and the Company claimed the right of appointing even local officials and it was strictly laid down that no appointment made without the permission of the Company was valid. These high-handed measures did not in any way lead to the pacification of the country. On the other hand even the Rajah surreptitiously encouraged the rebels and for a time the position of the Dutch in the fort became highly precarious. The commandeur Van Dielen who knew of the preparations of the nobles and the attitude of the Rajah kept Van Rheede, the Commissar-General, fully informed of the projects and the Company was seriously afraid that the high-handed policy of the Commandeur had undermined its position in Cochin itself. From this position they were saved and their authority further consolidated by the unwise action of Veera Kerala Varma whose decision to adopt from the Chaliyur family plunged the country into a civil war and helped to consolidate the position of the Dutch.

In 1681 Veera Kerala Varma, on the advice of Martin Huysman, the commandeur of Cochin, and of the Lord of Paliyam decided to adopt into the Cochin family two princes and four princesses from the Chaliyur Branch. This was not welcome to the Nayar nobles as the Chaliyur Branch had always been the dependents of the Dutch and under the lead of Ayinikkuttil Nambidi and the Treasurer, Perumbalam, they agitated against the proposal for adoption from Chaliyur, and suggested the adoption of princes from Vettathunad. This faction which was anti-Dutch had the support of the Rajahs of Mangat, Parur and

Manakkulam and the Madampies of Karappuram. When the Chaliyur adoption was actually made in 1689, these noblemen gathered their forces in Mangat and resolved on deciding the issue by force. The Rajah was by this move thrown into the hands of the Dutch Company. But even then the position of the Company was weak as the Rajah had not the support of the people of Cochin. None of the leading nobles of Cochin, except Ittinnan Achan of Paliyam was on the Rajah's side, and to champion his cause meant a land campaign of an arduous nature. On this occasion both the Company and the Rajah turned to the Zamorin. For his help in the Dutch conquest of Cochin the Zamorin had received only Cranganore and his further claims on Vaipeen were not accepted by the Company. Yet it was to him that the Company and the Cochin Rajah turned at this moment of crisis. The Zamorin who was then reigning was Bharani Thirunal who was born in 1640 and ascended the gadi in 1684. He was a ruler of remarkable ability, he was naturally unwilling to come to the help of the Dutch but the Brahmin ambassador of the Cochin Rajah was able to persuade the Nayar Chiefs that as Cochin had again accepted the authority of the Zamorin there was no necessity to keep up the age-long quarrel. The Commandeur also visited the Zamorin at Cranganore.[1]

Forgetting for once the historical role of the Zamorin, which was to resist foreign aggression and to support the popular cause in Cochin, which policy

1) Mamankodtharanam, p. 39.

successive Mana Vikramans[1] had followed with unfailing fidelity, the then Zamorin agreed to help the Company and the Cochin Rajah to defeat the Vettathunad faction. He was promised for this help the land of Chetwai and all military expenses. The Zamorin's army took the field immediately and joining the forces of Paliyam and of the Company marched forward to meet the rival army encamped near Alwayi. The Dutch forces were commanded by Hendrick Van Rheede who was Commissar-General. The opposing armies met at Alwayi, and the Vettathunad forces commanded by the Rajah of Mangat were defeated and dispersed. The war was carried into the enemy's territory but soon the Dutch retired with the plunder of the rich lands of Alangad and Parur. The Zamorin received Chetwai which he had so long coveted.

But in getting Chetwai the Zamorin had lost the historic leadership of Malabar. The fall of the Mana Vikramans may be traced to this campaign when for the first time in their long history they joined hands with the foreign powers and their vassal, the Rajah of Cochin, in order to put down a popular anti-Dutch rebellion. In the next serious campaign against the Dutch in 1717 the Zamorin was fighting not as the leader of Malabar and the head of its popular forces but merely as a powerful king. The war of Vettam succession was thus an event of utmost importance in Malabar history. It consolidated the power of the

1) Mana Vikraman is the name which the Zamorin adopts on succeeding to the throne.

Dutch at Cochin by making the Rajah completely dependent on the Company and by breaking the power of the anti-Dutch nobles. It saw the reversal of the traditional policy of the Zamorins, who so far had been the champions of the popular cause against the autocratic pretensions of the Cochin Rajah and the aggression of the foreign traders. By allying himself with his hereditary enemies, and those who were historically the enemies of Malabar freedom, the Zamorin lost at one stroke the singular position which two centuries of war in the cause of Kerala had earned for him.

The rivalry and feud between Cochin and Calicut were by no means at an end. The Zamorin, now well established at Chetwai and Cranganore, continued to encourage Cochin feudatories to create trouble in the Rajah's territories and to support the different factions in the country. Though nominally there was peace, the Cochin Ruler was particularly angry that the Zamorin had not evacuated the territory occupied by him during the late war. The argument of the Calicut government was that the agreed contribution to its military expenses in support of the Cochin Rajah had not been paid. Desultory warfare went on in which the Zamorin was generally successful, especially because strategically he was so placed that Calicut armies could always be moved with ease into the Cochin territory while his own domains were free from attack. The Dutch who were anxious to maintain peace with the Zamorin took up an attitude of neutrality. In fact they were not displeased at this continual warfare between Cochin and Calicut as it kept the Cochin ruler occupied. The idea of Ravi Varma who had succeeded to the gadi of Cochin in 1693 was to embroil the Company with the Zamorin but the instructions of the Batavian Government and the policy of Hendrick Van Rheede who was Commissar-General were to avoid further complications with Calicut.

In 1694, the relations between the Rajah of Cochin and the Company became very strained. The Company's Indian Agent, Bavan Prabhu, was a corrupt official in the pay of the Zamorin and he sided with the young chief of Paliyam, Ittykkanachan, who had come of age and was intriguing with the Dutch against his own master. The Rajah was powerless especially as Isaak Van Dielen, the commandeur who was inclined in his favour, died a few months after the Rajah's accession. In a letter dated January 22nd, 1694, the Rajah complained bitterly of the attitude of the new Paliyam chief and of the irregularities of Bavan Prabhu, the Indian trade agent of the Company, in refusing to account to the government for the customs and duties of the port. He also accused the Prabhu of being in the pay of the Zamorin. To this complaint the Government of Batavia gave an evasive reply and told the Rajah that full instructions had been given to Adrian Van Maten, the new commandeur, and that the Rajah should consult him on all occasions. The Company in fact was anxious for peace with the Zamorin and took no heed of the complaints of a prince whose importance rested solely on their support. The activities of Bavan Prabhu and the Paliyam chief were in no way interrupted. Nor did the Commissar-General or the commandeur take up an attitude which was favourable to the Rajah. The unhappy prince sent a further petition in June 1696. In it he complained that though the Commissar-General, who was instructed to discuss matters with him, arrived at Cochin, he did not stay to have an interview with the Rajah but proceeded to Calicut where he saw the Zamorin and entered into friendly relations with him. Bavan Prabhu was also with the Commissar-General and this enraged the Cochin Rajah more than anything else. That the Company should not have supported him in his fight with the Zamorin was in itself galling to him but that they should, when hostilities were actually taking place between the Cochin Rajah and the Zamorin, go to Calicut and ostentatiously display their friendship was a matter which he could not suffer.

We get a glimpse of the state of Cochin finances at the time from this letter to the Supreme Government at Batavia. The Rajah complains that owing to the civil strife beginning with the last days of the Portuguese the state treasury has been left bankrupt. The only sources of revenue left to him were the mint, the customs, the profit on the private sales permitted on his behalf by the Company and the percentage on pepper. Of these the mint was run as a joint enterprise by the Company and the Rajah, and as the Dutch claimed from the state treasury a large sum of money, the profit from the mint was only credited to the account. Owing to the hostile attitude of Bavan

Prabhu practically nothing was realised from the customs and duties and the treasury was therefore bankrupt. The Dutch kept on pressing vigorously for the payment of their debt and at this crisis the Rajah Ravi Varma died to be succeeded by Rama Varma. With him a new agreement was made by the Company. This was negotiated by Hendrick Zwaadekroon in 1698, and it finally set the seal of servitude on the Cochin principality and made it merely an appendage of the Dutch Company.

By this time, however, the general monopoly which the Company had hoped to establish had broken down. The whole basis of the theory of compulsion was that the selling of pepper to other nations was contraband which was to be put down by the use of the Company's whole force. Unless the Company was able to inspire that degree of fear which would force Malabar rulers to proceed against their own merchants, this policy was bound to fail. This is in fact what happened. Zwaadekroon's memorial[1] shows how little the power of the Company was feared by the Rajah of Kayamkulam who traded openly with the pirate William Kidd, though the Company had negotiated with Goda-Varman, the Rajah of that place, so late as 1592, a treaty for exclusive trade in consideration of 500 gold fanams and the right of sending out a vessel of 75 or 100 candyles.

A great portion of the pepper produce of the country used to reach the English. The Governor-General writing to the Company's authorities at Amsterdam as

1) Dated 31st May, 1698.

early as November 17th, 1669 states "immediately after the conclusion of the peace with England the Agents of the English Company have again taken up their residence at Calicut. . . . . . We are much afraid that from the district of Thekkumkur and Vadakkumkur a large quantity of pepper will find its way overland to Calicut which will make this article dear."[1] All this reacted on the position of Cochin on whose ruler the Company had to put the screw mercilessly in order to make their settlement paying.

1) Dutch Records at the Hague—Vol. 29 DCCCXLI Page 6.

CHAPTER III

THE DUTCH WAR WITH THE ZAMORIN

The Zamorin's position had been considerably strengthened by the accessions of territory in 1663 and 1691. In 1663 the Dutch, agreeably to the treaty with Van Goens, handed over Cranganore to the Calicut ruler. In 1691 the Zamorin secured Chetwai for the support he gave against the Vettam faction. The two natural ways of attack on Cochin from the North were from Cranganore and from Chetwai and controlling these the Zamorin kept the offensive always in his own hands. Chetwai especially was of great importance because it lay in the domains of Payencherry Nayar, a feudatory of the Zamorin and a nobleman of considerable power and influence. The Ruler of Calicut built on the Cochin frontier a line of fortresses of which Pappanety, Kattur, Mapranam and Oorakam were the most important. Besides this, the Zamorin was in close alliance with the chiefs of Mangat and Parur whose principalities bordered on Cochin in the north and with Thekkumkur and Vadakkumkur the two powerful Nayar rulers occupying territory to the south of Cochin. Placed in this advantageous position, it was no more than a recognised sport for the Zamorin Rajahs to attack Cochin when they felt so inclined. So far the Dutch had preserved an attitude of neutrality and had shown anxiety for friendly relations with the Zamorin. In 1694 though there was possibility of a serious war between Cochin and Calicut, the Company maintained the attitude of a passive spectator. But the relations between the two Rajahs did not improve especially as the Cochin Rajah was anxious to get back Mapranam and Chetwai. Matters came to a crisis in 1700 and the Dutch, who were anxious not to be embroiled in war, asked the Zamorin to send his representatives to discuss the outstanding questions. They also invited the representatives of the Rajahs of Purakkad, Vadakkumkur, Marta and Parur to meet in Cochin and help to settle the matter by arbitration. But the Zamorin would not agree to this and on the 19th February 1701 he invaded Cochin territory. The Dutch Company decided to support the Rajah of Cochin and took the field with a large force. Nor was the Zamorin without allies. Purakkad and Parur declared for Calicut and the Zamorin by promising an adoption into his family from Thekkumkur got the support of that important state. The Purakkad Rajah carried war into the Cochin territory in Karappuram and thus created a diversion which helped the Zamorin a great deal. The Dutch Company finding itself attacked from the north and the south decided to buy off the Rajah of Purakkad and separate negotiations were entered into for that purpose. The crafty Brahmin chieftain after securing many advantages for himself retired from the fray.

But the war against the Zamorin was not progressing at all. The Cochin Rajah complained to Batavia that the Dutch Company were not serious in their efforts to support him and he claimed, by virtue of his treaties, full co-operation in the campaign from the supreme government. The reply of the Governor-General, Jan Van Horn, dated 15th November 1705, is of interest as indicating the lines of Dutch policy in Malabar. The Cochin Rajah had tried to arouse the fear of the Dutch by stating that the Zamorin was negotiating with the French Company for a settlement at Calicut and that if the Dutch did not support the Rajah "with soldiers, with ships and ammunition" his authority as well as theirs will cease to exist for ever. To this the Governor-General replied thus: "I do not know how much treasure and how much blood had been spent by the Honourable Company to aggrandise your family. But I know one thing. Our advice to put the affairs of the State in order has been uniformly disregarded by your Highness. Your Highness has lent your ears to the selfish counsels of Chetties, Nambudiries and Pattars; still the Company are not averse to give support to Cochin agreeably to our treaty but they will not at all times send their soldiers to fight your Highness's battles. For the last 50 years Malabar has been a source of large expense and little gain." But the Company at the same time seriously discussed whether it was not desirable to recapture the important line of fortress on the Cochin border and render the Zamorin's attack on Cochin impossible. After serious consideration the Company decided on actively supporting the Cochin forces in their attempt to recover Mapranam. In a letter dated 27th October 1707 the

Company claimed Cochin to be a protected state and gave the Zamorin to understand that attack on Cochin would be considered as a hostile act against themselves. The real reason for this action was not any particular friendship for Cochin but the negotiations that the Zamorin was carrying on with the English for the establishment of a factory in Calicut. The Zamorin's reply to the letter was of a conciliatory nature and the commandeur invited the representatives of all parties for a conference at the fort in Cochin. The conversations, though friendly, did not end in anything definite. The war between Cochin and Calicut continued and though pressed by the Rajah to help him the Company refused.

In the meantime things were taking a new turn at Calicut. At the Zamorin's court there were two parties. The Zamorin himself was a peace loving man who was desirous that this war should come to an end. But the great chiefs of the army, especially Dharmoth Panikkar, the heir apparent himself, and most of the nobles were in favour of continuing the war. The Mamankam festival[1] was approaching and as the position of the Zamorin as the leading King in Malabar depended on his taking the initiative in that matter he decided on peace and entered into definite negotiations. By the treaty which resulted from these negotiations the Zamorin handed over Chetwai to the Company. The Nayar Lord of Payenchery became a feudatory of the

1) The Mamankam was one of the great national festivals of Malabar. Originally it was a national assembly for the election of an Emperor for all Malabar. In its later days, the Zamorin assumed the control of this festival though the traditional forms of an imperial election were still kept up.

Dutch and the Cranganore Rajah also was given over to their protection. The Cochin Rajah gained considerable additions of territory.

This treaty did not find favour with the Calicut nobles, especially with the heir apparent and the Commander-in-Chief, Dharmoth Panikkar. They pointed out that in giving over Chetwai and Cranganore to the Company the Zamorin had disabled himself from taking the offensive in any future war and that if the Dutch Company began building a fort in either of these places it would be a standing menace to the kingdom of Calicut. Though the Zamorin recognised the validity of these arguments he was forced to remain quiet for a considerable time. But when it was found that the Dutch were not content with merely wresting those strategical areas from him but were actually fortifying Chetwai, he was naturally incensed and entered into negotiations with the English. Besides this, the Cochin Rajah anxious always to embroil the Zamorin with the Dutch handed over to the Company the legal title to some pieces of land which had long been in possession of the Zamorin. The Dutch took over the place and began erecting a strong fort in spite of the vigorous protest of the Zamorin.

The Zamorin was enraged at this high handed procedure.[1] The war party at his court utilised this for pushing forward their views and they found a friend in Robert Adams the energetic, if rather headstrong, English factor at Tellicherry. The English factor promised all help with munitions and money and

1) Visscher—Letter IV.

encouraged the Zamorin to act vigorously. Adams had strong reasons for taking this course. Not only did he desire that the Dutch power should be weakened by continuous fights with the Zamorin but he realised that special opportunities for pushing up the English influence would offer themselves if there was war between the two powers. Besides, Chetwai was a source of considerable income to the English Company as in that place they had established a branch house and carried on trade in opium which was a prohibited commodity in Cochin.

The Zamorin was not anxious to proceed by force. He protested at Cochin against the hostile acts and warned the Company of the disastrous consequences that would follow if they persisted in that course. But the commandeur took no notice. He ordered that the construction of the fort was to be proceeded with in as great haste as possible. There was no option now but war. But the Zamorin was still averse to a general campaign against the Dutch and wanted only the reduction of the two forts that were being constructed. In spite of the advice of the heir apparent and Dharmoth Panikkar it was decided that there was no necessity to proceed against the Dutch but merely to take by force the area, legally belonging to Calicut where, on the pretended conveyance of Cochin, the Dutch Company were building their forts.

The following is the description given by Visscher of the capture of the fort by the Zamorin. "The fort was now almost completed and he saw that the time for his attempt was come. He was encouraged by learning that the garrison consisting of 48 men were lodged outside the half finished fortress and that none of the requisites had been provided for its defence. This showed the greatest want of foresight in the Commandant who had received intelligence of the intended attack and ought therefore to have increased his garrison and ordered his men to keep within walls and to be alert. The Zamorin perceiving his advantage crossed the river at night with 600 men who were soon followed by more, and all was effected so quietly that at about 4 O'clock in the morning of 22nd January 1715 they surprised the soldiers who were sleeping in their huts before the fort."[1] In the face of this clear statement, the version of Hamilton, who was not in Malabar at the time, that the Zamorin first introduced some of his men under the disguise of labourers and that the surprise was successful only because the disguised labourers killed the sentinels, signalled to the ambuscade and attacked the half built fort, could not be true. If such was the case Visscher, who was chaplain in Cochin itself from 1717-1722, would certainly have mentioned it as the cause of the Dutch failure.

The action in any case was completely successful. The two Dutch lieutenants who were in charge of the operations were both, according to Hamilton, diverting themselves with a game at tables in a grand room about half a mile away. The moment the Zamorin's soldiers occupied the fortress the Dutch retired to a mud turret at a distance. The captain made no

1) Visscher—Letter IV.

attempt to recapture the fortress but ignominiously retreated to Cochin leaving the place in the hands of the Zamorin. He was immediately arrested, deprived of his commission and sent to Ceylon for trial. The commandeur of Cochin, Barent Kettel, immediately made the necessary preparations and with a large force backed by heavy artillery left Chetwai. He was met on the way by a detachment of the Calicut force under the Rajah of Mangat and a sanguinary action took place. Both sides lost heavily with the result that the Dutch army was not able immediately to attack the fortress. In the meantime, the Calicut general entrenched himself in a secure position and brought down heavy artillery. Kettel was in a difficult position. He had either to attack with the small force at his disposal or retire without fighting. His communication had become unsafe and the force which he had brought was insufficient to undertake a major operation against a fully equipped army. Retreat was even more dangerous. The communication by the backwater was threatened by the Rajah of Mangat. The commandeur decided to attack. On February 1 an attempt was made to storm the fortress, but the attack, though made with vigour, was easily repulsed with heavy loss to the Dutch. The Commandeur and what was left of the force returned to Cochin.

With Chetwai abandoned the Dutch position at Cranganore became precarious. The Rajah of the place hastened to return to his old allegiance and the Zamorin proceeded to erect a fortress at Pappanety between Chetwai and Cranganore with a view to resist any.

future attack of the Dutch on Chetwai. In December 1715 reinforcements were sent from Batavia with orders that Chetwai must immediately be recaptured. Commandeur Kettel, anxious to retrieve his failure, put himself to the task with energy and on January 11th, 1716 an attack was made. Even that patriotic chaplain Canter Visscher who was regaling his relations at home with the heroic deeds of his countrymen in the East had nothing good to say of this expedition. Says he: "Owing partly to some misunderstanding among the officers and partly to the faint-heartedness of Captain Pluis, the second in command, who trembled at the sound of cannon, the attempt failed. For, when the besieged beheld our men advancing, they were so terrified at their numbers that they rushed out of the fort on the opposite side. Those of our troops who were stationed there, mistaking the cause of the sally and imagining it was an assault upon themselves were seized with a sudden panic and fled in disorder. The fruitless result of the expedition created universal consternation which was increased by the rumours which began to fly about mostly originating in the apprehensions that the allied princes were about to desert us."[1]

The loss of Chetwai and the failure of two successive attempts to retake it constituted the greatest blow that the prestige of the Dutch arms had so far suffered in India. It was a disaster that spelt the ruin of their trade and the disappearance of their political influence. The council at Batavia realised that unless

1) Page 17.

their prestige was regained, every one of the small chieftains would turn against them and defy them with impunity. Urgent orders were therefore issued to concentrate on Malabar as much troops as possible. In September, 1715, no less than 1570 men were sent to Cochin. In 1716, 1500 more were sent. The force was well supplied with arms and ammunition. This was probably the largest European force concentrated in India before the rise of British military power.

The Dutch established a blockade of the Calicut coast. On the 15th June 1716 a vessel flying the English flag laden with munitions of war but carrying also English passengers was captured by the Dutch. It must be said here that the policy of the Dutch Company towards the English on the Malabar coast was never friendly, as we have seen in the Purakkad case. "Every means must be employed and effort made", wrote the authorities at Amsterdam in a letter dated 14th May 1667, "to have the English expelled from the land of the Zamorin. . . . . It will never do to have that nation settled so near us".[1] From November 1669 the English Company had established a factory at Calicut. The English factor at Tellicherry who had general control over the English establishments on the coast heartily reciprocated the sentiments entertained by the Dutch. The capture of the English ship gave Robert Adams the opportunity he wanted. He claimed from the Dutch restitution and compensation. The Dutch commandeur did not answer his communication and

1) Dutch Records at Hague Vol. 29 CCXLI. (India Office).

Adams sent another insolently worded protest and accused the company of grossly ill-treating the English passengers captured with the ship. On the 14th July, Barent Kettel made a counter protest saying that in allowing munitions to be imported into Calicut, Adams was acting in an unfriendly spirit and the Dutch had every right to capture ships belonging to the Zamorin even if they were flying the English flag. Adams was not to be suppressed in that manner. He replied that even if the ship belonged to the Zamorin the Dutch had no right to capture it as long as it flew the English flag. This bitter controversy, interesting in itself to show what sides the English Company took, did not interfere with the course of action. The army had by this time been collected from all parts of Dutch India. Hendrick Zwaadekroon who was commissioner for Malabar in 1697 and who as such had earned a great name with the princes was offered the command, but he refused. The Council then made William Baker Jacobs, who held the position of Councillor Extraordinary, Commander-in-chief.

Jacobs arrived in Cochin on the 16th November, 1716. Barent Kettel was recalled and Johannes Hartenberg was appointed in his place. Jacobs made no secret of the immense preparations the Company had made to carry on the war to a successful conclusion. He addressed an official letter to all the kings and nobles of Malabar declaring that he had been sent out to punish the Zamorin and humble his power. Jacobs did not know how a boasting Marechal of Portugal had undertaken to do the same two hundred years before and had met with his death at Calicut, and that a greater man than he, Alfonso Albuquerque, had to confess that, in spite of all his efforts, the power of the Zamorin remained unbroken because it was based on the loyal allegiance and the willing co-operation of the Nayar nobility. However, Jacobs announced his intention with much flourish.

The Dutch commandeur marched on Chetwai. He took with him the whole of the formidable force which had been mobilised at Cochin during the last year and a half. The army at his command contained, besides the Nayar force supplied by the Rajah of Cochin, 3226 Dutch soldiers and 193 lascorins. The attack on Pappanety was personally conducted on the Zamorin's side by Dharmoth Panikkar and by Jacobs on the Dutch side. A most sanguinary battle took place in which the superiority of the Dutch artillery soon became evident. It was clear that the fortress could not withstand effectively the cannonade of the Dutch batteries and the Calicut force after a stern resistance evacuated it by the evening. The Zamorin also withdrew his forces from Chetwai.

The campaign, however, did not end with this. Desultory fighting continued and after some time the armies again met for a decisive battle at Oorakam where an overwhelming Dutch force of over 25,000 men consisting of 15,000 Cochin auxiliaries and 5,000 Dutch soldiers overtook a portion of the Zamorin's army. The battle continued for the day but the result was indecisive. The Zamorin's forces withdrew from the field and negotiations were opened for a treaty.

The Dutch on their side were not anxious to continue the war. The war had cost them already two million guilders and had strained their military and financial resources to the utmost extent. Their gains in the campaign were comparatively small. They had, it is true, defeated the Zamorin in pitched battles, but his army was intact and his territory inviolate. So far the campaign had been conducted in Cochin territory and in the disputed soil. The Zamorin was also weary of warfare and was prepared to negotiate a suitable peace. But the Dutch demanded heavy indemnity which the Zamorin was not prepared to pay. The negotiations thus dragged on. In the meantime, through the intervention of Cochin, the Company entered into agreements with some of the marcher barons who had so far supported the Zamorin. Of these the most important was the Chief of Punnathur, who agreed to desert his king and abide by the orders of the Company.

After considerable time spent in fruitless negotiations a definitive peace was made with the Zamorin (1717). The Zamorin agreed to pay the nominal indemnity of 85,000 gold fanams. The Dutch also insisted that Dharmoth Panikkar, who was according to Governor Moens "the chief firebrand of the treason of Chetwai" should be dismissed and that his property in Chetwai should be forfeited to the Company[1].

---

1) This property is situated at the northern limits of Pappinivattam in the neighbourhood of Tripporayar temple and consists of 50 acres of sowing land and 63 pieces of garden land. The revenue from this is called in campaigns documents as the Revenue of D'Hermuttu Panikkal.

The Company and its servants were given the right of trading within the territories of the Zamorin. The Company withdrew its claims on Punnathur Nambidi. Payenchery Nayar whose lands were situated in the area between Cranganore and Chetwai was recognised to be a vassal of the Company. Pappinivattam (Pappanety) was given over in full sovereignty to the Company. Chetwai was formally taken possession of on the 10th April 1717.

Thus though the campaign ended in favour of the Company, the benefits derived did not by any means justify the enormous expenditure or fulfil the objects with which the Dutch began the War. The Zamorin's power was not materially crippled, nor was he "punished" in any manner. Though the Company annexed Pappanety, and the fortress at Chetwai, the enormous expenditure of two million guilders, which the campaign entailed and the interference with trade to which it led, became more a punishment to themselves than to the Zamorin.

All the indemnity which the Dutch received from the Zamorin was the insignificant sum of 85,000 fanams equal to about Rs. 30,000. The Cochin Rajah and the Dutch were soon to find that neither the strength of the Zamorin nor his power for offence had in any way been lessened by this.

CHAPTER IV

INTERNAL INTERVENTION

After the peace with the Zamorin, the Company felt that their position was established securely and that they could now stand forth as the overlord of the Malabar Coast. So far as they were concerned this claim of overlordship meant mainly an enforcement of the pepper monopoly and the right to purchase it at their price. They had put forward political claims only in Cochin. In that place they stood in the position of a feudal overlord. The Rajah of Cochin had become their bondsman by successive agreements which we have traced in a previous chapter. Johannes Hartenberg had even forced the Cochin Rajah to agree that "all the Rajahs, Princes and nobles of the kingdom shall lay their complaints and disputes before him so that he is constituted arbitrator between them by which means he becomes acquainted with their differences." Even the Civil Lists of the Cochin Rajah and of the princes were settled by the Dutch. By the treaty with the chieftains of Karappuram negotiated at Aryat on 6th April 1710, the Dutch secured very large powers of intervention in that area. But elsewhere the position of the Company was only those of merchants who had a monopoly of trade. At Purakkad and Quilon they had strong establishments which helped them to dictate to the Rajahs but in neither place did they have any effective political power.

With the defeat of the Zamorin at Chetwai the vision of the political conquest of Malabar dawned on the Dutch. They were finding that the English at Tellicherry, Calicut and Anjengo, and the French lately established at Mahe were successfully breaking through their monopoly and getting a considerable share of the pepper trade of Malabar. The only way of tightening the hold on pepper was to reduce the other princes of Malabar to a position similar to that occupied by the Rajah of Cochin. The Zamorin whose influence had so long stood in the way of the Dutch was for the moment rendered powerless to act in an aggressive manner. Nor were occasions wanting which gave the Dutch opportunities for effective interference. The Rulers themselves invited such interference.

In May 1710 the Cochin Rajah addressed a letter to the Batavia Company[1] in which he complained that as a result of the open contempt in which he was held by the commandeur no one in the state paid any heed to him. "Considering the relations that exist between the company and the State I suffered with good grace all the humiliations in the belief that a remedy will soon be forthcoming." He appealed to the Governor-General to secure the succession of his immediate nephews in the Chaliyur branch to the Gadi after his time. He stated "They seem to be fit to be brought up to the status. . . . . The friends and

1) Recently published from the records of Paliyam by the state archaeologist of Cochin.

allies of my family hope that these boys would be adopted and request us to that effect. If they are not taken into this family no one can help them. . . . Those from Vettom being inimical to me and to the Company could not be trusted. The three princes at Ainoor are not in my opinion fit for the Stanam (title). Moreover some of them have been adopted into the Murianattu Nambiar family and are therefore said to have lost caste. They are quite unfit. If they are adopted the state will be ruined by selfish people." On these grounds he recommended that the Company should permit him to bring into the Cochin family three more princes from Chaliyur.

Soon after the Calicut war was over, de Jong was sent from Cochin to Purakkad, Kayamkulam, Madathumkur and Quilon, ostensibly to make new contracts but really to make the Rajahs understand the new position of the Company. But even without such official notification the Rajahs were able to draw their conclusions when the company interfered on the ground of *illegality* in the adoption made by Murianattu Nambiar.[1] Claiming the rights of a Malabar overlord the Dutch declared the adoption made by the Nambiar to be invalid and threatened to proceed against him if he proved himself contumacious.

But in all these the Dutch had calculated without their host. The Zamorin was soon in a position to take up the leadership of Malabar and in 1728 he suggested to the Thekkumkur family the adoption of a princess to Calicut. This would have meant a definite check to

1) Press List No. 134. Letter to Batavia.

Dutch intrigues in that area and it would also have isolated and enfeebled Cochin. Vadakkumkur and Thekkumkur belonged to the same family and their open alliance with the powerful ruler of Calicut meant nothing less than the annihilation of Cochin. The Zamorin however did not stop with this. He was moving in the direction of a Malabar confederacy against the Dutch and their vassal the Rajah of Cochin. The Dutch resident at Kayamkulam, Johannes Batta, reported in 1729 that the Zamorin had sent *Olas* (letters) with a Brahmin ambassador by name Padmanabha Pattar to the King of Kayamkulam asking him and the Rajah of Thekkumkur to attack jointly the Rajah of Cochin from the south in order to facilitate the Zamorin's policy.

De Jong's overbearing attitude towards the princes had raised a host of enemies against him, and the Zamorin's combination was an ominous portent of the discontent in Malabar. The Dutch realised this and recalled de Jong from Cochin in 1730. A combination between the Chieftains of the north and south of Cochin would have crushed the political power of the Dutch which was centred at Cochin and ruined their trade especially as Cochin itself did not produce in any considerable quantity the articles that the Dutch wanted. So de Jong's policy was for the time reversed and a conciliatory attitude was taken up towards the allies of the Zamorin in the south.

There was another reason for the change. A new complication had arisen in the question of succession to the Mangat principality, which affected the Dutch.

directly. The domain of Mangat lies to the North-east of Cochin and comprises of the present taluk of Alangad (in Travancore) and lands adjacent to it. Its position is such that it covers the only important land frontier of Cochin if the little Brahmin principality of Idapalli is left out of consideration. The Chiefs of Mangat were Nayars and owed allegiance to the Zamorin, whose generals they claimed to be. They were lords of 16,000 Nayars. The Cochin Rajah had also vague claims of overlordship which the Mangat Nayars never accepted willingly. It was the Chief of Mangat who led the Zamorin's forces on the occasion of Barent Kettel's attack on the captured fort of Chetwai in 1716. In 1730 there were only two members in this family, the Chief himself, and the heir apparent who had been adopted from the family of Murianattu Nambiar in 1728. But as the perpetuation of the line demanded the adoption of a Rani—the Mangat family being matrilineal—the Rajah decided on adopting a lady from the house of Koratty Kaimal, another Nayar lord of equal standing. The heir apparent objected to this and put forward the claims of his own sister, a lady from Murianattu Nambiar's family. Matters came to a crisis in 1733. The prince rose in revolt against the Chief and in this action he had the support of the Dutch who supplied him with arms and ammunition. The Dutch Company were by no means desirous of peace in Mangat and it suited their purpose better to see that state weak and disunited. The Rajah of Cochin supported the cause of Koratty and clandestinely helped the Chief against the prince. The whole matter was referred to the arbitration of the Dutch commandeur and the Rajah of Cochin. As a result of their mediation an agreement was reached on the 8th July.

The award was in the nature of a compromise. The Chief was to adopt the sister of the heir-apparent as the first princess, and the lady from the Koratty Kaimal's house as the second princess. The debts incurred by the prince were to be paid off, but the prince was to return the state treasures in his possession and surrender to the Chief his arms and ammunition. A further clause stated that no future adoption would be valid which did not get the previous sanction of the Cochin Rajah and the Dutch Company. The prince refused to accept the award and to give up the guns in his possession. The civil war therefore continued and the position necessitated constant vigilence on the part of the Company.

Nor were affairs elsewhere going any better. The Rajah of Vadakkumkur was assassinated in 1733 by the heir-apparent and a civil war had broken out there also. The prince next in succession asked the Dutch to mediate in the quarrel. In 1734 Tottassery Thalachennor or chief was murdered in the Trichur temple. The Rajah of Kayamkulam was at war with the chief of Maruthurkulangara, and there was continuous warfare between the neighbouring chiefs of Parur and Mangat. The hand of the Dutch Company was only too apparent in all this.

The Dutch had also at this time to face considerable trouble in North Malabar. The English who had established themselves at Tellicherry came to an agreement on the 2nd November 1730 with the Regent of Kolathiri, who at that time was at war with the Rajahs of Cannanore, by which the Company received a monopoly of trade in Iruvanad, Dharmapatam and Randathara. The English trade greatly increased by this. At this time the Canarese who were at war with the Kolathiri also invaded Malabar and came up to Valarpattanam. The Dutch suffered greatly from this attack but held aloof from the combination of Malabar princes organised by the Regent with the help of Stephen Law who was the English factor at Tellicherry. But when the expedition against the Canarese began to progress satisfactorily the Dutch joined it on the understanding that the English will do nothing to intercept their trade to the north of Cannanore. On the 1st April 1736 the Canarese forces were attacked and routed and their General, Gopalji, slain. The Dutch, however, did not persist in the campaign and fell out with their ally the Regent of Kolathiri. The reason was that the Dutch wanted the prince to sell them 1000 candies of pepper at a fixed price. The Kolathiri had maintained even in the early days of his connection with the Portuguese that the sale of pepper was not his business but that of private merchants. Finally in January 1737 the prince agreed to sell 1000 candies of pepper at Rs. 56 per candy and the Dutch agreed to help him in the war.

The French at Mahe were also intervening in political affairs. War broke out between the Iruvanad Nambiars and the French in 1739 and the latter had the worst of it. In 1739 and 1740 French arms suffered numerous reverses in North Malabar. This was but the prelude to a greater effort. In November 1741 de Labourdonnais arrived with two ships at Mahe and attacked Kadathanad and defeated the Rajah's forces. But peace was concluded satisfactorily to all parties and the French and the English settled down amicably. This was a further blow to the Dutch.

Elsewhere the policy of intervention continued. The company itself did not interfere in the fights between the princes for the simple reason that it would have been a costly pastime for a trading corporation. They got the Rajah of Cochin to do this work for them and that Chief under the illusion that his power would increase by such intervention was never loath to play the *agent provocateur* for the Dutch. Their policy on this matter was no secret. In a letter dated 8th October 1735 the Supreme Government at Batavia directed the commandeur at Cochin that care should be taken that the Zamorin and the Rajah of Cochin do not become friends; that incidents which would lead to the continuance of unfriendly relations between the two states must always be created. This policy they carried on with the different princes and noble families of Malabar with the result that all of them were continuously engaged in warfare thus becoming more and more dependent on Dutch help. Circumstances looked so favourable at that time that the Company decided on territorial conquest on a small scale. So far they had confined their military commitments principally to Cochin. When, however, they saw how well they had succeeded in spreading anarchy in Malabar the vision of standing forth as one of the chief Malabar powers came to them. In the secret letter to Batavia dated 12th May 1741[1] it was communicated that the decision was taken to annex Anji Kaimal and Maruthurkulangara. Portions of Vadakkumkur were also to be conquered and the strip of territory from Colachel to Cape Comorin was to be occupied. In fact ever since Van Imhoff's arrival in Eastern waters visions of this nature were floating before the Company. Van Imhoff was, like Albuquerque, a born imperialist. Gustaf Wilhelm, Baron Van Imhoff, belonged to one of the most distinguished families in the Netherlands. He came out to Malabar in 1725 at the early age of 20. In 1732 he was sent again as councillor extraordinary, and in 1736 he became ordinary councillor. In 1737 Van Imhoff arrived in Cochin to report on Cochin accounts. The unsatisfactory financial position of the settlements on the Malabar coast had long been a source of concern to the Supreme Government and they had on numerous occasions suggested that the authorities at Cochin should not interfere in political affairs and should retrench their expenditure. Van Imhoff after a thorough examination of the situation came to the conclusion that compulsion should be used to get the Rajahs to fulfil strictly the commercial terms of their agreement and sell to the Company at stipulated prices the whole quantity of pepper. This was no easy matter. It meant an increase in the military establishment of the Company. Van Imhoff also conceived the idea of

1) M. S. No. 335.

conquering portions of Malabar and holding them as direct estates. There was an important reason which convinced him of the necessity of this action and that was the growth of British trade in Malabar. We have seen how, as soon as the Dutch were firmly established in Cochin, they got the English expelled from Purakkad and every method was used to dislodge them from Calicut. The Zamorin, however, encouraged the English to stay. The influence of Robert Adams at Calicut and the increasing trade of the British factory at Anjengo were political complications of considerable magnitude. Robert Adams was a forceful individual, more of a political adventurer than of a commercial agent. He gained very considerable influence over the Zamorin and his intervention was felt seriously by the Dutch in the wars with the Ruler of Calicut. "In consideration of the assistance given at Calicut and money given to my servants" the Zamorin gave Adams additional privileges in 1710. For the help in the campaign against the Dutch he received a concession to build a fort at Chetwai. With nothing at his disposal but his own very considerable wits he built up a great political reputation for his country. He made Zamorin friendly to the English and the trade of the Dutch suffered greatly by this. As, however, the treaty of 1717 restored Chetwai to the Dutch, Adams had to retire to Tellicherry.

At Anjengo in the South, the English were established more firmly. In 1684, the Rani of Attungal allowed the Company to settle for trade, and in 1690 permission was given to build a fort. The local nobles did not approve of this grant and in 1697 they combined to attack the fort while the Rani herself gave support to the factors. In 1694 the Tellicherry factory was established in the territory of Kolathiri. In 1708 the Tellicherry fort was formally made over by the Vadakelemkur or the Northern Regent of Kolathiri.

In 1721, the factory at Anjengo suffered a great disaster. The factor who had been invited to Attungal to present his annual Nuzzur went with unnecessary military display and the Nayar Chieftains suspecting an invasion attacked him and cut his escort to pieces. In 1723 Alexander Orme concluded a treaty on behalf of the English East India Company with the Rajah of Travancore. The Rajah wanted to erect a fort at Colachel for which the English Company was to supply the artillery and munitions. The treaty also declared that the Rajah was to be in league and united in good friendship with the East India Company. It is interesting to note that this is the first treaty negotiated by the English East India Company with an Indian State which is now in existence. As a result of this treaty the Company's position on the coast improved and their trade in pepper and spices developed greatly. They supplied artillery and munitions and received pepper, cardamom and other spices in exchange.

The growth of the English trade in pepper and piece-goods and the slow but sure rise in their political importance and the arrival of the French at Mahé made the Dutch realise that the game of playing off one ruler against another could now be played by the Malabar rulers against the European Companies. The English could be set against the Dutch; the French could be set against both. For this reason, as also for the political complications in Java, the Dutch were unable to act vigorously at the time when they could have asserted their political authority. Instead of this they tried the game of nibbling interference and created against themselves a host of enemies through the length and breadth of Malabar.

CHAPTER V

THE RISE OF TRAVANCORE

Up to the accession of Martanda Varma in 1729 Travancore was only a minor principality and did not count as a factor in the general politics of Malabar. Though the Trippappil family is undoubtedly ancient as is witnessed by the fact that one of its members attests the copper plate grant of Vira Raghava Chakravarthi, its influence in Malabar politics in the days of the Portuguese and in the first fifty years of the Dutch connection was very little owing to the subdivision of its territory and the internal squabbles of the different branches of the family. Travancore was but one of the five branches into which the Trippappil family was divided. The others, Deshinganad or Quilon, Elayadath Swaroopam, Attungal which was ruled by the eldest princess of the family and Nedumangad were often at war with each other and with Travancore. The principality itself extended only from Edavai to Thovala. The southern portion of this territory both climatically and to some extent ethnologically belonged to the Tamil districts, and its political and cultural affiliations were more with Madura and Trichinopoly than with Calicut, Cochin and Quilon. There was also another and more immediate reason for the negligible influence of Travancore before the 18th Century. In Travancore, more than anywhere else in Malabar, the feudal nobility had reduced royal power almost to a vanishing point. By a settlement made in 1050 A. D. the Government of the Sripadmanabha Temple at Trivandrum which owned most of the lands in the country was handed over to a council consisting of eight hereditary Brahmin priests and the Rajah. The Rajah, however, was to have only half a vote. This ecclesiastical commission was given full authority to collect the revenues and administer them. The councillors or Yogakkar divided the area owned by the temple into eight districts over each of which they placed a nobleman entrusted with the collection of revenues. In course of time these noblemen known as the Lords of the eight Houses—Ettuveetil Pillamar—usurped all secular authority. With the encouragement of the Temple Yogakkar they partitioned the territory. The Rajah became a mere figurehead. During the reign of Rajah Aditya Varma who ruled from 1661 to 1677 the feudal anarchy in the State took the most violent forms. The palace of the Rajah was set fire to and later on the ruler himself was poisoned. As there remained only a Rani named Uma Amma with her six minor children, the nobles succeeded to all the power in the State and paid but nominal allegiance to the Ruler.

When this state of anarchy was at its height a Moghul soldier of fortune appeared in the South with a small force of cavalry. Meeting with no opposition he advanced on Trivandrum and established his authority in its neighbourhood. The Rani herself retired leaving the capital to the invaders. The nobles who had usurped the royal power made no attempt to organise opposition. The Rani, however, rose to the occasion and invited the help of a prince from Kottayam in North Travancore, Kerala Varma by name renowned alike for his prowess in the field as for his literary and artistic accomplishments. He was not slow to respond to the desolate Rani's call and organising a small force from the adherents of the family drove out the invader and freed the country again. But Kerala Varma was not allowed to enjoy the fruits of the victory. With the disappearance of the Mohammedan adventurer, feudal anarchy revived and Kerala Varma was assassinated in his palace by the agents of the Ettuveetil Pillamar.

The next few years saw the culmination of this state of anarchy. The Rajah himself was a fugitive and the nobles had everything their own way. It was at the height of this anarchy that Martanda Varma was born (1706). While he was but fourteen he vowed like Philip Augustus of France that he would re-establish royal power in the state and put down the might of the nobles. From that time, even while he was only a prince, twice removed from succession, he set himself with single minded devotion to the task. Soon the Pillamar found out that they had to deal with one who was as ruthless as they were and more determined than they. Naturally, all their power was directed towards his destruction. For many years the prince was a fugitive, chased from place to place, escaping from the clutches of his adversaries only through the steadfast loyalty of the peasants. His experiences at this period taught him that if the anarchy which reigned in his state was to be put down, it could only be done with the help of a powerful military organisation. It was soon clear to him that if he depended on raising a local militia for this purpose he could not succeed because the Nayar system of military organisation was based on service to the immediate feudal lord and not to the sovereign. So in 1726, while still heir-apparent to the throne, Martanda Varma advised his uncle to take what was the most important decision in the history of Travancore, to offer his allegiance to the new Moghul Governor of the Carnatic and solicit his help for the extermination of the refractory feudatories. With this object the Rajah left for Trichinopoly accompanied by a few leading officers of the State and paid homage and allegiance to the throne of Delhi, which, in spite of the wars that followed Aurangazib's death, was still the Empire of India—in the person of its Governor of the Carnatic. He agreed to pay a tribute of 3000 rupees to the Nawab of the Carnatic who in exchange took him under his protection. In the eyes of the Moghul Governor, the Rajah of Travancore was no more than a petty ruler and the treaty concluded between the Nawab and the Rajah, speaks of Rama Varma as a Zemindar of Malabar. But what was lost in dignity was more than compensated by the effective force put at his disposal. The Rajah returned to Travancore with an army of 2000 infantry under Tripathy Naicker, and

1000 horse under Venkitapathy Naicker. This army with which it was hoped to crush the nobles and establish royal authority was to be paid by the Rajah and was to remain under his orders.

Martanda Varma succeeded to the throne in 1729. Though only 23 years old he had learnt both warfare and statecraft in the school of adversity. With the help of the Carnatic troops he set himself out first to crush the nobles. But he soon found that these soldiers of the Nawab would not take their orders from him and were in the position of his masters. They arrested and imprisoned his minister and in other ways showed that they owed no allegiance to him. Nothing daunted Martanda Varma set to work at once to raise an army of his own. Within the short time of a few months the Rajah raised and trained a Maravar army with which he replaced the forces lent by the Nawab. But even with this new force Martanda Varma did not find matters easy. Sri Padmanaban Thampi, the son of the late Maharaja, claimed the throne and appealed to the Nawab of Arcot as the Suzerain. The Nawab as well as the Travancore nobles supported his claim. An army was sent against the Rajah who, however, was able to bribe the commander and get him to retire. The Thampi and the Pillamar, thus betrayed by the commander of the Trichinopoly forces, were left alone to face the wrath of the Rajah. But even unaided, the strength of the nobles was such that Martanda Varma did not dare to attack them openly. In 1733 the Thampi who was the head of the faction was assassinated while on a friendly visit to the Rajah and the nobles were also surrounded and arrested at the same time. Clemency was not one of the virtues of Martanda Varma and the vengeance he enacted was of a nature that struck terror through the whole of Malabar. Forty-two of the proudest nobles were sentenced to be hanged and their women and children were given away in slavery.

This was the first and the most important blow struck against the Malabar political system. With it went the feudal conception of Malabar polity. The old idea was that the Nayar lords could not be punished even in case of treason. In fact, as pointed out in a previous chapter, the Dutch Company made it a condition in their treaty with Cochin that the Nayar nobles who rebel against the State should be punished. Though the Company had demanded it, the Cochin Rajah had been unable and perhaps unwilling, as too revolutionary a procedure, to punish his noblemen who were constantly in revolt against him. Martanda Varma swept away those notions of chivalry and exterminated without scruple the families that had so long dominated the state. He wished to found an autocratic state such as was in existence at Trichinopoly and at Tanjore. The conception was entirely foreign. The instruments used for its realisation were equally foreign being the mercenary army of Maravars recruited on the East Coast.

With all internal opposition crushed with so little difficulty Martanda Varma turned his attention northwards. The area immediately to the North of his own state was partitioned between the Rajahs of Quilon and Peritaly (Elayadath Swaroopam). Martanda Varma had already found occasion to intervene in their affairs on the ground of adoptions against his interest. The Quilon Rajah had in 1731 decided on an adoption from the family of Kayamkulam. Martanda Varma demanded that this adoption should be rescinded and on refusal attacked Quilon with a large force. The fort of Quilon was very ably defended by Atchuta Variar who was the chief minister of the Rajah. Though Variar fought with great gallantry he had to yield to superior strength. Quilon was annexed and the Rajah was interned at Trivandrum as a state prisoner. This was the first occasion in which a state was thus dealt with in Malabar history, for until this time, the custom was merely to reduce the ruler of a conquered territory to the position of a subordinate chief and leave him in the enjoyment of his territory.

This annexation of a historic principality, naturally spread consternation in the rest of Malabar. The northern princes immediately organised a confederacy to liberate the Quilon Rajah and install him again on the throne. The minister of Kayamkulam, Easwara Pattar, went to Cochin to persuade the Company to take the leadership in this alliance. But the Dutch authorities in Cochin had not yet recognised the full significance of Martanda Varma's policy. The quarrels between Malabar chiefs were by no means unwelcome to them as it only strengthened their hold on all. The new warfare meant to conquer and to annex had not entered their calculation, nor had they counted on the force of the military system which Travancore was slowly introducing in the place of the inefficient feudal hosts of traditional Malabar warfare.

The Northern Alliance which the Kayamkulam Rajah negotiated met with some success, in spite of the lukewarm support given by the Dutch. The Rajahs of Kayamkulam, Procaud, Vadakkumkur and Cochin agreed to support each other in a war against Travancore the object of which was to re-instate the Rajah of Quilon on his throne. The Rajah of Maruthurkulangara who was not in the coalition was to be attacked and the forces of the allies were to invade and reconquer Deshinganad. The Rajah of Quilon who was interned in Trivandrum successfully escaped and reached Kayamkulam. A strong force was placed at his command and he immediately marched on Quilon. The Travancore garrison commanded by Arumugham Pillai put up a stout resistance but was obliged to retreat. The allied forces gained another notable success against the main body of Travancore forces led by Martanda Varma himself. The Quilon Rajah was safe again on his throne and the allies carried warfare into Travancore territory.

Martanda Varma had retreated merely in order to remedy the defects in his military organisation and had no intention of giving up the fight. He reorganised his army, especially the new cavalry, procured more efficient weapons and trained and drilled his forces to a point up to which no other Malabar prince had done. The English merchants at Anjengo and Edavai sold him new and improved war material. When the military reorganisation was complete Martanda Varma took the field again. He divided his forces into two armies and simultaneously attacked Kayamkulam and Quilon. The campaign against Quilon met with immediate success; but at Kayamkulam, the Travancore army was again defeated. Every time the forces of Martanda Varma came out in open conflict, they were heavily defeated and driven back. By an accidental shot the Rajah of Kayamkulam was killed on the battlefield in 1734, but his brother who succeeded him carried on the campaign. Martanda Varma was forced to own defeat and retire.

Defeated ambition again turned to foreign aid to achieve its purpose. For the second time in his short reign Martanda Varma tried to raise a corps of foreign mercenaries with whose help he could conquer Malabar chieftains. Ramayyan—an intriguing and unscrupulous Brahmin who had gained the confidence of Martanda Varma—was deputed to arrange with the Polygars of Tinnevelly for a Marava force. Ramayyan secured the services of Ponnam Pandia Tevan, a Marava chief, who brought with him one thousand horses. With the help of this new reinforcement Martanda Varma made another attack on Kayamkulam. Though he gained some minor advantages in the campaign the military power of Kayamkulam remained unbroken and a treaty was made by which peace was re-established and the Rajah of Quilon was reinstated on his throne. But the Travancore Rajah had no intention of remaining at peace. In 1734 he annexed Elayadathu Swaroopam, a principality lying to the east of Quilon. The unfortunate Rajah of Quilon also died in this year and this precipitated the third war with Kayamkulam.

On the death of the Quilon Rajah, the chief of Kayamkulam claimed the territory by virtue of adoption and immediately took possession of it. Martanda Varma, who had already protested against this adoption and refused to recognise it, claimed the territory for himself. War seemed imminent, when the Dutch Company, who had already begun to feel nervous at the restless ambition of Martanda Varma, intervened. Commandeur Maten sent an envoy to Martanda Varma remonstrating against the annexation of Elayadathu Swaroopam and warning him against attacking Kayamkulam. Martanda Varma, who at this period of life seems to have been absolutely ignorant of the position and power of the Dutch and had not introduced these unknown factors in his calculations for the conquest of Malabar, was surprised at their action. His experience of European merchants was practically confined to the English at Anjengo who did not interfere in political affairs and whose only interest lay in trade. He did not evidently realise at the time that the Dutch claimed political suzerainty over some portions of Malabar and were preparing to enforce it by arms in the coastal region. Martanda Varma's ignorance on this point was useful on this occasion. He sent a reply to Maten in which he asked the Dutch Company to mind their own business and not interfere in the politics of Malabar. This reply naturally incensed the Dutch. The internal difficulties of the Dutch in Java made an immediate attack on Travancore impossible and this gave Martanda Varma his opportunity to make extensive preparations for the new war with Kayamkulam. Ramayyan, who had in the meantime become Prime Minister and Commander-in-chief, marched against Kayamkulam in 1739. The Dutch considered this to be a proper time for intervention. Van Imhoff, the great Governor of Ceylon, was then at Cochin and he decided to take immediate action. The treasury in Cochin was, however, not in a state to undertake any great military responsibility. So as a first step Van Imhoff decided that the princes and chiefs who were bound by agreement should be forced to yield the full quantity of pepper and those who were unable were to be mulcted of large sums. Van Imhoff also decided that Marta and certain provinces of Vadakkumkur should be conquered and annexed to the Company's territory. In the meantime a messenger was sent to the Rajah of Travancore asking him to reinstate the princess of Elayadathu Swaroopam but Martanda Varma was in no mood to listen. Van Imhoff himself undertook a journey to the court. He was received with every courtesy but all his diplomacy could not shake the resolution of the Rajah. Van Imhoff threatened and cajoled in turn; but Martanda Varma proved obstinate. They were, indeed, well-matched. The Dutch Governor was a man of extraordinary personality, great courage, and in every way a leader of men. He was determined to gain his point by methods of peace, and failing them, by methods of war. By long experience of diplomacy and warfare in the East, Van Imhoff knew the price he would have to pay for a prolonged campaign in the Travancore hills, away from the range of his ships' guns. But he knew also that if he allowed Martanda Varma to defy him on a matter on which the Dutch were bound alike by their treaty obligations as by their own interests, then the Company would have every petty chief in Malabar against it. Martanda Varma was also equally obstinate. Of his courage and resourcefulness the Dutch had already ample evidence. He did not realise the might of the Dutch on the seas; but as his reply to Van Imhoff proved, he was well aware that he had all the advantages on his side in a prolonged campaign of guerilla warfare conducted from an impregnable base on the hills. War between two such adversaries was therefore inevitable.

Van Imhoff's plan of campaign was well conceived. He decided upon attacking Travancore simultaneously from the north and the south. A powerful force well equipped with artillery was to land at Colachel from Ceylon and conquer the area between the Cape and that port and march northwards. From Quilon another force was to attack Trivandrum, while the Rani of Elayadathu Swaroopam, reinstated in her state, was to attack Martanda Varma from the east. As a price of her reinstatement the Company received Vechoor. Martanda Varma did not wait for the campaign to open. He recognised that the weakness of Van Imhoff's plan lay in the untrained levies of the Rani and therefore directed his attack against her. The forces of Elayadathu Swaroopam were completely routed and the Rajah re-occupied the territory. In the meantime the Ceylon forces landed at Colachel. The Rajah who had expected to finish his northern campaign in a short time in order to be ready for this invasion found himself in a hopeless position. The Dutch forces soon fortified their base at Colachel and from there systematically conquered the area to the south of it. Martanda Varma was forced to abandon his northern campaign and proceed south to meet this new menace. But it was a hopeless situation that faced him. The Dutch had established themselves firmly in the littoral from Cape Comorin to Colachel and were advancing on Padmanabhapuram which was one of the chief cities in the state. In this state of despair Martanda Varma turned to the new power which had risen in the Carnatic—to the French at Pondicherry under M. Dupleix. Negotiations for an alliance were entered into with the French, who were only too glad to get this opportunity to interfere decisively in the affairs of Malabar. But before the new alliance could be of use the fortune of the war turned in the Rajah's favour. Martanda Varma even in this most desperate plight had not abandoned his hope or given up the struggle. He had enlisted and trained a new army which was fully supported by an efficient arm of cavalry and with this force he attacked and totally defeated the Dutch at Colachel (10th August 1741). The Dutch abandoned their positions and evacuated Colachel itself, leaving many persons wounded and 24 Europeans as prisoners. A quantity of muskets fell into the hands of Martanda Varma when the fort was occupied by him.

The battle of Colachel was, in its effects, a disaster of the first importance to the Dutch. It is true that the struggle itself, like that of Plassey, was hardly anything like a big battle. But it put an end to the Dutch dreams of the conquest of Malabar. It was the first great blow inflicted on the Dutch arms and its moral effect was so great that the Dutch never recovered from it at all. They were too powerful on the sea to yield immediately; but from this time, except for unimportant diplomatic skirmishes with Travancore, the Company was reconciled to the position of mere traders without political pretensions.

So far as Travancore was concerned the battle of Colachel may be said to be the most decisive factor in its development. It removed the main obstacle in the way of its triumphal march towards the north and made the conquest of Kayamkulam and other states possible. As long as the Dutch barred the way and declared that they were the allies of the minor states, Martanda Varma was cooped up within his narrow boundaries. But the victory of Colachel made such an intervention impossible. It also increased the prestige of Martanda Varma with the rest of the Malabar princes. Till 1741 his arms had achieved no great victory. His fight with Kayamkulam had been indecisive. At Quilon "the gallant old Rajadorai Atchuta Variar" had held him at bay. Nowhere had he made any headway. But this victory showed the Malabar princes that Martanda Varma had not only the ambition but that he also commanded the power to conquer the rest of them.

Of the 24 prisoners taken at Colachel there were two lieutenants, Eustachio D'Lannoy and Doncaud, a Frenchman, whom the Maharaja selected for employment in his army. After his experience of the East Coast Martanda Varma had realised the value of cavalry as an arm of his military force. The war with the Dutch taught him the superiority of trained infantry over the feudal levies of Malabar. He employed these two officers to organise for him a standing army trained and armed on the western model. D'Lannoy[1] was useful for the Maharaja in the construction of an arsenal and the provision of an efficient magazine. These activities put the state of Travancore on a new footing and made it possible for it to expand northwards.

In the course of 12 years Martanda Varma had suppressed rebellion in the State, uprooted the elements which had so long rendered the kingdom impotent, annexed Quilon and Elayadam, defeated the Dutch and established unquestioned power from Kayamkulam to Comorin. Now he had organised an efficient standing army and created for himself an instrument which was powerful enough for the purpose of welding Malabar into a single state. Within this short time he

1) De Lannoy's tombstone can still be seen in Udaigiri fort. It bears the following inscription:—

Hic iacet Eustachius Benedictus de Lannoy qui tanquam dux generalis militiae Travancotidis praefuit ac per annos XXXVII ferme summa felicitate regi inserviit cui omnia regna ex Caimcolum usque ad Cochin vi armorum ac terrore subjecit. Vixit annos LXII menses V et mortuus est die Junii M D C C L XXVII. Requiescat in pace.

had also undertaken numerous reforms, some of a very expensive kind—like Nanjinad irrigation works—and made the state not only the most powerful but the most progressive of Malabar kingdoms.

CHAPTER VI

THE EXPANSION OF TRAVANCORE

After the defeat of the Dutch at Colachel Martanda Varma was free to attack his enemies in the North. The only serious enemy who was powerful enough to hold up his advance was the Rajah of Kayamkulam. Supported by a powerful and well disciplined army the Maharajah marched against that state. The three previous campaigns undertaken against that state had not the effect of breaking its military power and Martanda Varma found that the Rajah was ready to win or die but would never yield. Of all the minor principalities to the south of Calicut, Kayamkulam alone had the tradition of heroism, which for centuries had resisted all attempts to encroach on its territory or to curtail its independence. The new attack on Kayamkulam developed into a desultory campaign. The Dutch who felt the disgrace of the defeat of Colachel gave every help to the Rajah of Kayamkulam who counter-attacked Travancore territory and laid waste the lands of Marta, a state which Martanda Varma had already annexed. In 1742, the Dutch fort of Quilon was attacked by the Travancore soldiers but there they suffered a crushing defeat at the hands of the gallant old "Rajadorai Atchutha Variar".

The armies of the Kayamkulam Rajah advanced from Quilon into Kilimanoor, a town of considerable importance, not far from the capital itself. The

Kayamkulam forces captured the fort and made preparations for advancing further south. But at the height of his misfortune Martanda Varma showed courage. He mobilised all available troops within striking distance of Attungal, recruited a new army and spent his last penny in equiping the forces at his disposal by arms and ammunitions procured from the English at Anjengo and from the French at Mahe. Martanda Varma was fighting clearly with his back to the wall. If he lost the battle he stood to lose everything. The Kayamkulam army with their Dutch allies could, if victorious, march straight to Trivandrum. But never did Martanda Varma's courage shine better than in adversity and the blind goddess favoured him. He surrounded Kilimanoor and besieged the Dutch and Kayamkulam forces within the walls. After a siege of 68 days the Travancore forces carried the fortress by assault and the commandeur of Cochin and the Rajah of Kayamkulam retreated to Quilon. But the defeated army was not given time to reorganise. Martanda Varma was quick to press an advantage and the allied forces of the Dutch and Kayamkulam Rajah were chased to the walls of the latter's capital. Defeated again in open conflict, the Rajah signed a separate peace and became a tributary of Travancore and ceded to Martanda Varma more than half his territories.

With Kayamkulam under him, Martanda Varma's career of conquest met with no serious opposition. Vadakkumkur and Thekkumkur were immediately attacked and after a short campaign annexed to Travancore. A more serious campaign was necessary to subdue the Rajah of Purakkad. As soon as Kayamkulam was annexed, Martanda Varma entered into negotiations with the prominent leaders in the Purakkad State with a view to weaken its defences. That state was one of the mainstays of Dutch power on the coast and the Rajah of the place was a loyal ally, first of the Portuguese and now of the Netherland Company. If the Dutch power was to be broken on the coast, it was necessary that the Rajah's dependence on the Company must first be destroyed. The Minister of the Rajah, the Bhattathiri of Thekkedam, and the general of his forces, Mathur Panikkar, visited or sent delegates privately to the Maharajah. But before hostilities were actually begun, the Dutch Company sent a message that they were prepared to negotiate for peace. The continued warfare in Kayamkulam, Quilon and Vadakkumkur had caused much loss to the Company's pepper trade. Not only were they involved in considerable military expenditure which burdened a depleted treasury but even the ordinary trade of the Company suffered owing to the conquest by Travancore of Quilon, Kayamkulam and Vadakkumkur. Naturally, therefore, the Company was anxious for peace and made direct overtures. The minister Ramayyan and Talavady Kochumoosad were sent by the Maharajah as plenipotentiaries to meet the Dutch representatives, Ezekiel Rabbi and Captain Sylvester Mendes, at Mavelikkaray. But as both parties put forward claims which the other would not accept, the negotiations came to nothing. The Dutch were not yet so completely defeated as to be forced to surrender their dominant

10*

position, and Martanda Varma had gained too much political sense to allow them to meddle again in Malabar political affairs. The Company wanted to be considered a political power; Martanda Varma would negotiate with them only on the basis of their being a trading agency.

Negotiations were started again a few months later only to be broken off and desultory conversations were kept up as neither side cared to carry on actual war. The reason of this peculiar diplomacy was that Van Imhoff was in the Indian Seas with an imposing armada and whenever he came near the Malabar coast, the Maharajah took up a conciliatory attitude. But the Dutch, if they thought they could intimidate Martanda Varma by a demonstration of imposing naval strength, were totally mistaken.

Though the Dutch did not embark on direct hostilities, they did not hesitate to build up another coalition against Travancore. The Rajah of Kayamkulam, who found the conditions imposed by Martanda Varma too irksome for his independent spirit, was easily persuaded to take up the leadership of this new confederacy which included the Rajah of Tekkumkur and Purakkad. A new war broke out and Martanda Varma's forces marched north in 1746. Kayamkulam was taken and the territories belonging to its ruler were permanently annexed. Now Martanda Varma was free to turn against Purakkad. The Purakkad Rajah of that time, according to Gollenesse, was a young man of about 35, of great intelligence and some ability. His state was difficult to attack and conquer as it was a marshy area. Also, his army was highly trained and well equipped. The Travancore army was opposed by the Rajah's forces at Tottappalli—the southern extremity of his state and in the battle that ensued the Purakkad army remained victorious. But the crafty Brahmin Minister, Ramayyan, was equal to the occasion. He entered into negotiations with the general of the enemy's forces, Mathur Panikkar, who was bought over to the Travancore side. For this disgraceful betrayal the Panikkar was rewarded by grants of title and money. After thus buying off the main portion of the Rajah's troops, the Travancore forces again attacked and turned the Purakkad lines. The Rajah himself was taken prisoner and sent to Trivandrum.

From out of the six Dutch establishments south of Cochin, Quilon, Marta, Kayamkulam and Purakkad thus passed under the control of Travancore. The agreements which the Dutch had made with those chieftains for the monopoly of pepper trade became valueless and the Company soon recognised that with a hostile Travancore their trade in pepper and cardamom would continue to fall. Malabar in fact had become a serious drain. The area to the north of Cochin which after the successful war with the Zamorin in 1717 was yielding excellent results in pepper trade had again become a cockpit of warfare. The Zamorin invaded Cochin in 1742 and took possession of the great temple of Tripproyar. After a great deal of desultory fighting in which the Cochin Rajah suffered much loss, the Zamorin, taking advantage of the Company's difficulties with Travancore, attacked Chetwai. The Payencherry Nair, a former feudatory of the Zamorin, whose allegiance was transferred to the Company by the treaty of 1717 joined the Calicut forces. The whole area of Chetwai was reconquered. Thus, attacked from both sides, the Company decided that peace with Travancore was an immediate necessity. The draft treaty submitted by Travancore was ratified in 1758 (15th Aug.) though its provisions had in the main been accepted and carried out in 1748. This treaty which practically destroyed the political power of the Dutch in Malabar deserves careful study. The main clauses are that the Travancore Ruler undertook on any pretext not to receive or encourage other European powers in the territories subject to him provided that the factories of the English at Anjengo Vizhinjam and Edawai may be allowed to continue; if any other European power attacked the Maharajah the Company will give full support by land and by sea.

The Maharajah undertook to deliver to the Company 1,509,999 lbs. of pepper every year at the price of Rs. 65 per candy. The English Company should receive only as much as they are entitled to by the treaty of 1727. But it was also agreed that the Travancore Rajah would sell to the Dutch at the cheaper rate of Rs. 55 per candy pepper from countries which he had conquered or will in future conquer. The most important clause, so far as Travancore was concerned, was that the Dutch undertook not to interfere in favour of any one with whom Martanda Varma and his successors were at war. The Company also undertook to sell war material at cost price to Travancore.

Two important facts will be noticed with regard to this treaty which places it on a different footing from all the previous treaties concluded by the Dutch.

Firstly, the Dutch Company surrenders all pretensions of political authority and undertakes not to intervene in favour of any prince attacked by Travancore. The extent of this surrender will be realised only when it is remembered that the cause of the war between the Company and Travancore was an attempted intervention by the commandeur of Cochin in Quilon and Elayadath Swaroopam. The Dutch Company had always claimed that except in the case of the Zamorin of Calicut they had the right of intervention and that they were the final arbiters in all disputes. We have seen how they insisted that they should be consulted, and their permission taken, for adoption in the families of Mangat and Parur. In Cochin they had gone even so far as to declare themselves direct suzerains. With most of the states they had treaties of alliance which put on them the burden of defending the Rajah from external aggression. Their surrender of this claim was therefore a perfidious betrayal of their allies who had put their trust in them. By this, the Dutch Company handed over the petty Rajahs of the coast to Martanda Varma whose military power, based on a Marava force recruited from Tinnevelly, was irresistible in their eyes.

The disastrous implications of this clause were pointed out by the Cochin Rajah in a formal protest which he lodged with the Supreme Government at Batavia. He complained that the company had "sacrificed an old friend and ally besides other Malabar kings and broken all contracts. When from the very beginning our ancestors tried to bring some kings under their sway and obedience the Honourable Company continuously interfered; by observing this rule this kingdom got divided in so many parts and has, therefore, become unable to check its powerful enemies. Now that the king of Travancore has become a powerful king he has been able to coax the Honourable Company under promise to observe everything by means of which he bids fair to bring the other kings under his sway. But we believe he will shortly try to subjugate the Honourable Company also and besides it will have to put up with all kinds of affronts in one way or another."[1]

The second point of importance is that this treaty contains no clause about special protection for Christians. Ever since the first Portuguese treaty made with Quilon the European traders had taken the Latin Christians of the coast under their special protection. These people were tried and punished by the Company and they had their special privileges guaranteed. This extraordinary system was the cause of much trouble and when Martanda Varma refused to include it in the general clauses, the Company, having had to yield on even more important points, was not strong enough to resist.

There is no doubt that the first of these two exceptional conditions dealt the death blow to the Company's position on the coast. The stipulation that the Com-

1) Qaoted in Cochin State Manual, Govt. Press, Ernakulam, pp. 108-109.

pany shall recede from all engagements which they may have entered in with other Malabar princes whom the King of Travancore may choose to attack and that they will on no account interfere in their disputes or afford them assistance or shelter was indeed too humiliating a surrender to have been made for nothing. The Dutch had suffered no crushing military defeat under pressure of which they were compelled to sign this clause. Though the campaign had gone against them, their military position was safe and unassailable. What was then the motive behind so fundamental a surrender as this clause implied? The fact was that the Dutch had lost the pepper trade as a result of the war and were anxious to secure it again. In 1726 they had exported 1,952,979 lbs. of pepper. In 1746 when they were at war with Travancore the quantity had been reduced to 541,189 or almost to ¼th. This was a grievous loss and the Batavian government realised that if their trade was to be re-established in Malabar, it could only be done by one of two methods: either by reducing the king of Travancore to a tributary chief or by coming to an agreement with him. The first course was found to be impracticable. There was, therefore, nothing more to do than to accept the best terms for their trade. The Company besides securing from the ruler of Travancore an agreement to sell annually to it 1,500,000 lbs. of pepper at Rs. 65 from his ancient territories, also got better terms for pepper from the territories to be conquered by him. From the point of view of trade they gained greatly; for during four years 1756-1760 they collected 10 million lbs. of pepper or an average of two and a half millions a year.

The treaty clearly ended the Dutch political power. Even in the matter of trade the benefits secured by the treaty for the Dutch proved to be temporary. When the Travancore Rajah had conquered the petty chiefs and extended his territory up to Cochin, he denounced the trade clauses of the treaty and when reminded of his obligations to sell the Company pepper at a fixed rate he gave them the crushing reply that as they no longer had any political power they were only merchants and as such the Maharajah would be glad to give them permission to buy in the open market.

With the Dutch neutrality thus established by the treaty, Martanda Varma was in a position to advance towards the North. That was easy enough. Thekkumkur and Vadakkumkur were conquered and the boundary of Travancore extended from cape Comorin to the Periyar river. But the people of Kayamkulam, Purakkad, Changanachery and other northern principalities, so long accustomed to independence, and the feudal nobles, so long masters in their own houses, rose up in revolt against this invasion of Tamilians. The Travancore conquest was not really the conquest of one Malabar State by another. It was the conquest of Malabar States by a ruler who had made himself strong by the help of Marava mercenaries. The Rajah of Purakkad escaped from his internment, and took up the leadership of this movement. He was joined by the other dispossessed rulers of Vadakkumkur and Thekkumkur and received also the assistance and active support of the Cochin feudatories. The Cochin Rajah himself had become nervous about his position between the Zamorin and the Maharajah of Travancore and therefore joined the alliance. Martanda Varma had foreseen this probability. He had already launched upon a diplomatic offensive against the Rajah of Cochin by encouraging the factions in the Cochin family which were against the Ruler. In the Cochin family there are two titles, Perumpadappu Muppil or the head of the family who is the eldest member of the ruling and non-ruling branches combined, and the Ruler who is the head of the ruling branch. In 1748 these two dignities became separate as the eldest member who claimed the title, Perumpadappu Muppil, belonged to the dispossessed branch. The Rajah, however, refused to recognise the title. The disinherited prince escaped to Trivandrum and sought the help of Martanda Varma, who was not slow to recognise the diplomatic value of this claim. He took the prince under his patronage and notified the Cochin authorities through the Company that any settlement made without his concurrence would not find acceptance.

The chronicles of Trippoonittarah mention that there was another cause of conflict between Cochin and Travancore. Martanda Varma had taken possession of the rich and ancient temple of Tiruvalla which was under the control and sovereignty of the Cochin Rajah though it was situated in Travancore. Naturally the Cochin Rajah was incensed and he thought that the new combination gave him an opportunity of humbling the proud Rajah of Travancore. The Vadakkumkur

Chief kept back from the alliance as a result of his connection with the dispossessed Cochin princes. But the coalition looked formidable. The Cochin army was commanded by Palliyil Idikkela Menon, the Paliyam Chief being a minor at the time. The campaign went against Cochin, though no serious engagement took place and the Rajah agreed to the terms suggested by Travancore. Cochin agreed to pay an indemnity, to accept the dispossessed princes and to surrender the land of Karappuram extending from Cochin to Alleppey to be ruled by them. The rulers of Cochin and Travancore met at Mavelikara in 1758 to negotiate a treaty and Martanda Varma was able to get these and some more important clauses agreed to by the Rajah of Cochin. It was agreed that all the pepper in Cochin—excepting 500 candies must be given up to Travancore, that the rights of the temples at Tiruvalla, and Haripad should be surrendered to Travancore, that the rights of the Princes should be settled after consultation with the nobles, and that Travancore should be given an indemnity of Rs. 25,000.

This treaty, however, was not ratified. The escape of the Rajah of Purakkad and the rebellion of the peoples of the newly conquered territories seemed to the Rajah of Cochin to afford a new opportunity for taking his revenge. The nobility of Cochin was particularly anxious to stop the progress of Travancore. The Dutch also secretly supported them. In a letter dated October 9th 1756 the Government at Batavia wrote to the Cochin Commandeur remarking that it was not possible to accept quietly the march of Travancore to the North and that he hoped action would be taken to ensure the success of the northern allies. A powerful Cochin army led again by Palliyil Idikkela Menon took up its position near the present town of Alleppey. The Cochin hosts were reinforced by the subjects of the princes of Kayamkulam, Purakkad and Vadakkumkur. This was in fact the last great fight undertaken by Cochin—the last field where the Cochin flag flew. The great noble families of the States were all there. Komi Achan,—the new heir of Paliyam, a brave and handsome youth of 18, but even in that early age giving the promise of highest distinction in war and statecraft, the personification of the feudal chivalry of latter day Malabar—, the chief of Kodassery, the Kaimal of Panamukkam, the Changaramkoda Kaimal, the president of the 30,000 of Tottachery and the rest of the great families of Cochin, forgot their ancient rivalries and took up their position besides Palliyil Idikkela Menon in an attempt to stem the tide of Travancorean aggression in which they saw not only the ruin of their own position but the conquest of Malabar by a prince whose main sources of strength were an alien bureaucracy of Tamilian Brahmins and a mercenary army of Maravas. But against the discipline and training of the Travancore forces their patriotism counted but for little.

The Cochin army reached Purakkad by the sea and took up its positions in December 1753. A small force also marched through Karappuram and joined the Cochin army. The Travancore forces immediately cut off their communications from behind and de Lannoy's artillery threw their whole army into confusion.

The flower of central Malabar chivalry fell on the field. Among those who were captured were the heir of Paliyam, the third Kaimal of Panamukkam and the chief of Kodassery.

The victory was systematically followed up. The whole of Karappuram was conquered and the Travancore army reached within two miles of the Dutch fort. The Rajah of Cochin sued for peace and the Dutch Governor strongly supported him and promised to act as an intermediary. But though the army of Cochin was defeated the people of Purakkad, Thekkumkur and Vadakkumkur were not so easily reconciled to the new Ruler. They rose again in revolt. The whole country north of Kayamkulam took up arms against the exactions of Ramayyan and the unchivalrous attitude of Martanda Varma towards the princes. The position of Travancore was precarious; but Martanda Varma in his desperation was utterly unscrupulous and totally devoid of all sense of patriotism. In order to put down the discontented populace he did not hesitate to invite the assistance of Hyder Ali who was then the Commander at Coimbatore. This policy of invoking foreign help to build up his personal greatness was at the root of Martanda Varma's policy from beginning to end. It is that which takes away from him any claim to greatness as a King of Malabar. The fact that he should have thought of invoking the aid of Hyder Ali to put down the discontent of his own subjects is the measure of his political sense as well as of his patriotism.

Fortunately for Travancore this remedy, more

disastrous than the disease, was not found necessary. The people showed a greater appreciation of the crisis than the King and peace was restored. But it is important to remember that much of the later misfortunes of Travancore arose from this foolish and unpatriotic act of Martanda Varma. Hyder Ali's assistance once sought was not so easy to shake off. He wrote to Martanda Varma that he was ready to march on the disaffected population of Travancore, but as the rebellion had quieted down the Maharajah declined Hyder Ali's assistance. The Mysore commander demanded compensation and considered the excuses of the Maharaja specious. The attack of Tipu on Travancore at a later date and the disasters that followed it were the outcome of this invitation.

The weakness of the Cochin Rajah and the loss of the Company's political power afforded the Zamorin the opportunity he was long waiting for to recover the areas he had lost to the Dutch. The reigning Zamorin was a prince of great ability and foresight. He was anxious to make the best use of the opportunity to recover Chetwai and in 1755 he attacked the Company's outposts at Pappinivattam. It will be remembered that by the treaty of 1719, the Zamorin had given up to the Company his feudal rights over the Velost Nambiar and Pazhayancherry Nair. The lands of these noblemen were also attacked and reconquered. The whole of the southern lands bordering on the backwater soon returned to the old allegiance. The Zamorin garrisoned the fortress well, strengthened the bastions and erected a new outpost at Pullikkarai with the object of cutting off the communication of the Dutch garrison at Chetwai with the sea. The fort at Enamakkal was surrendered to the Zamorin and the guns were taken to Pulikkarai for strengthening it. Chetwai was invested with 8000 soldiers. Calicut forces also occupied Parur and in May the Zamorin himself occupied Trichur. In October the outpost at Mulloorkarai was occupied.

The Zamorin then attacked the territories of the Rajah of Cochin. Having obtained the submission of Mangat and Parur the Calicut forces marched into Cochin from that side. Another army attacked from the side of Chetwai. The frontier on this side was controlled by the Enamakkal fort which was powerfully garrisoned with men and heavy artillery. But the commander of the fort surrendered it to the Zamorin without firing a shot. With Enamakkal in hand the whole of north Cochin lay open to the Zamorin. The feudal lords of the area offered no resistance and the rule of Calicut was firmly established. With his base in the heart of the enemy's territory the Zamorin advanced on Paliyam and occupied the domains of that chief.

In the short time of nine months the Zamorin had conquered practically the whole of Cochin and recovered the possessions lost by his predecessors to the Dutch. The Company tried hard by diplomacy as well as by force to get the Zamorin to withdraw from Chetwai. Commandeur Cunes himself went to Cranganore and the Cochin heir-apparent reached Tiruvanchikulam with an army. The chief of Paliyam commanded the main army. The effort so made to relieve Chetwai ended in defeat. The Dutch force was compelled to retire abandoning its artillery. With the field cleared of the Dutch soldiers, the Zamorin immediately attacked Cranganore. With a view to surround the territory of that chief the Calicut forces occupied Parur and then began to advance steadily on the fort of Cranganore. When matters came to this crisis the authorities in Cochin took fright and decided on determined resistance. But with the forces at their command no resistance was possible. The garrison in Ceylon was also below strength and as a result commandeur Cunes was helpless to take any effective action. In this plight he requested the lords of Chetwai to join hands with the Rajah of Cranganore and stop the onward march of the Zamorin. But these nobles instead of playing the commandeur's game decided to throw in their lot with the Zamorin and the Company was made to realise that they had ceased to possess the status of even a third class political power in Malabar.

The Zamorin's attack on Cochin almost annihilated that Kingdom. The Ruler of Calicut first secured the submission of Mangat and Parur. From there the Zamorin consolidated his rule over the area immediately in line with the new boundary of Travancore.

But at the height of his victory the Zamorin died on the 5th of May 1758. He was one of the greatest kings that royal line produced and in his time the glory of the Manavikrama Rajahs was redeemed. He was succeeded by a prince who was anxious for peace. It was feared that Hyder Ali would take an early opportunity to invade Malabar. The Zamorin was anxious to conserve his forces to resist this invader. The Zamorin was also getting anxious about the expansionist policy of Travancore. It was clear that, if matters were allowed to take their course the fight for Malabar supremacy would have to be fought out between Travancore and Calicut. It was necessary for this purpose that the Dutch should remain neutral and with this object in view the Zamorin made a treaty with the Company.

The progress of Travancore from the South made the position of Cochin equally impossible. Travancore had already occupied Karappuram and the territories lying immediately to the south of the capital. The Cochin Rajah was left with but a bit of territory but even over this the Travancore ruler put forward claims. It was at this time that Martanda Varma died (1758). There is no doubt that for all his shortcomings he was a great Ruler. It is no doubt true that he was unscrupulous, cruel to the point of inhumanity and unmoved by a sense of patriotism. He showed himself during the whole of his career entirely devoid of a feeling for Kerala Dharma and the basis of his statecraft was the utilisation of foreign help for subduing the chieftains opposed to him. Twice in his career he sought the help of foreign states to strengthen his own position; the second time he went to the extent of inviting Hyder Ali to come to his help in North Travancore. His cruelty towards the family of Ettuveetil Pillamar and the murder of the Thampis show that he attached but little value to fair play towards his enemies. Apart from these, from the point of view of Malabar history Martanda Varma's policy was disastrous in another way. His attempt was to sweep off the whole Malabar polity and establish in its place an autocracy of the type which prevailed in Madura under the Nayaks and in Trichinopoly under the Nabobs. This autocratic state was to be supported by the twin pillars of a mercenary army and an alien bureaucracy, both hostile to the population of Malabar and unsympathetic towards its institutions. The Travancore state was in fact a Tamilian conception and its advance towards the North was the victory of Tamilian over Malabar culture. Martanda Varma in the interest of his dynastic ambition surrounded himself with scheming Tamilians of whom Ramayyan was the supreme type and with ambitious adventurers like de Lannoy.

Even with these limitations it can hardly be denied that the results achieved by Martanda Varma were of a nature which give him a position in the front rank of Indian statesman in the 18th century. When he came to the throne his state was one of the smallest in Malabar. Royal power was practically non-existent. There was no money in the treasury. The army obeyed the commands of rebellious nobles and his own life was in constant danger. In Malabar politics the Dutch Company put forward pretensions of suzerainty and claimed the right to intervene in all affairs. In a few years' time he changed the whole map of Malabar. The Dutch Company was forced to abandon its proud position and had to be content with that of mere traders dependent on the goodwill of the Travancore Ruler. The minor principalities from Cochin to Quilon were all conquered and annexed and the rule of Travancore established firmly over them. An efficient and trained army was raised which gave to Travancore a predominance in Malabar affairs which no State had enjoyed before. Great irrigation works, roads and canals of communication were undertaken and carried out. Charitable institutions were founded. These results could not have been achieved except by a man who possessed rare foresight, strength of will, energy and decision. He was thus with all his faults the greatest Ruler of the Travancore line.

CHAPTER VII

THE ECLIPSE OF THE DUTCH

Among the prisoners taken at the great battle of Purakkad was the young heir-apparent of Paliyam, Komu Achan. He was sent to Trivandrum where he was kept in honourable confinement. Being of noble presence and high accomplishments the young prince became a favourite at the Trivandrum Court. His stay at Trivandrum helped to open his eyes to the new situation in Malabar and made him realise the strength of the forces operating in favour of Travancore. He realised first of all that the strength of Travancore as against the other Malabar princes lay in the fact that the unruly feudal nobility which considered warfare a hobby and changed sides to suit the occasion was crushed by Martanda Varma and in its place a trained army disciplined in modern manner was raised and maintained. He also realised that in the establishment of the central power of the state as against the pretensions of minor principalities lay the source of Travancore's greatness.

The scales fell off from his eyes also in regard to the Dutch. At Cochin the Dutch still looked a formidable power. They had their forts and their ships. But only the dilapidated facade of the once mighty edifice of Dutch power now remained. Its weakness was not visible from Cochin. From Trivandrum it was evident. To Komu Achan this came as a revelation.

The tradition of his family, as well as that of Cochin Rajahs was an alliance with the Dutch against the encroachment of the Zamorin. The Dutch were clearly enough powerless to resist the Zamorin and Komu Achan quickly grasped that Cochin would soon vanish into nothingness unless a valuable ally was secured. The chief of Paliyam, Kunjunnattachan, died soon and Komu Achan returned to Cochin as the hereditary Prime Minister of the State and the Ruler of his own fief.

From the first he had decided on his policy. He saw that for Cochin the only course of safety lay in an alliance with Travancore in its fight against the Zamorin. With this object he worked both at Cochin and at Trivandrum. He induced Martanda Varma to visit the Rajah of Cochin at his capital in November 1756, but the Cochin Rajah would not agree to cede any territory. The negotiations proved abortive. But Komu Achan was not made of the stuff which gave up a policy merely because it did not prove successful in the first instance. In 1757 the Cochin Rajah visited Trivandrum and a general alliance of friendship was then negotiated. When the Zamorin's attack on Cochin carried everything before it and Trichur and the areas around it were under the effective occupation of the Calicut ruler and nothing but a slice of territory was left for the Rajah of Cochin, Komu Achan succeeded in cementing a new alliance with Travancore. The chief of Paliyam came to Trivandrum in 1760 and negotiations were opened for a permanent treaty of alliance between the two states. The main clauses of the treaty were that Travancore was to send an army to drive the Zamorin out of the territories belonging to the Rajah of Cochin as a price of which the Cochin Rajah renounced all his claims over Karappuram, and agreed to cede to Travancore Alangad and Parur. If territories not belonging to Cochin were conquered from the Zamorin such conquests were to go to Travancore. The treaty was solemnly ratified before the altar of Sthanumurti at Suchindram.

Rama Varma, the new sovereign of Travancore, was anxious to continue the ambitious policy of his uncle. A gifted scholar and poet, a liberal patron of all arts, a musician and actor of renown, the Maharajah was also gifted with rare insight in political matters and combined high statesmanship and knowledge of foreign policy with a desire for active reform within the state. Unlike Martanda Varma he was a prince in the true tradition of Malabar chivalry. Kind-hearted and refined he stood out among the princes of his time as an exemplar in many ways. His fame spread to many countries. He is the Rama Rajah of whom the French, English, Mysorean and Carnatic correspondence speaks. Though averse to war, he had inherited the ambitious policy of his uncle which had as its object the unification of Malabar under one flag. The offer of alliance with Cochin[1] opened out a new line of action for him and he was not slow to take advantage of it.

The Travancore army marched forward under the command of the chief minister, Martanda Pillai. A

1) For the text of the correspondence see the Appendix.

small force was also sent by sea to Ernakulam. The plan of campaign was extremely well conceived. Trichur, in many ways the most important town in Cochin and its religious capital, was under the occupation of the Zamorin. The objective of the Travancore forces was to capture it, because the Zamorin's prestige in Cochin depended on his possession of this important town. Besides this, the strategic position of Trichur on the nodal point was such that it commanded all the routes and cut the territory of Cochin into two unequal portions and confined the Rajah to his coastal tracts. On arriving at Parur the Travancore commander on the advice of General de Lannoy decided upon a direct attack on Trichur from two sides. For this purpose the army was grouped in two divisions, one under Martand Pillai and the other under General de Lannoy. The plan was to make a converging attack on Trichur, the minister marching directly on it while the General was to capture Chetwai and attack it from the north.

The Zamorin's forces at Trichur were caught within the blades of this scissors; but from this difficult position the ruler of Calicut extricated himself by ordering his garrison at Chetwai to fight desperate rear-guard actions in which every inch of territory was resisted. In the meantime the Zamorin himself after a pitched battle which ended indecisively retired with his army in tact. The Calicut forces evacuated the Cochin territory and the Zamorin made peace with Travancore. The Travancore Rajah was glad to agree to an immediate peace. That the Zamorin in spite of the fact that he had suffered no heavy defeat sued for peace, was due to the exigencies of external policy. The growth of the Mohammadan power in Mysore and the aggressive intentions of Hyder Ali towards Calicut had made the fight with Travancore seem like a domestic quarrel. The clouds were gathering thick on the eastern horizon and the Zamorin was not slow to realise that the threat to his independence which the European fortress at Cochin meant and which had caused him 250 years of warfare with the Rajah of Cochin had ceased to be of importance and that the new source of danger arising from the military power of Hyder Ali was likely to succeed where Marshal Coutinho, Affonso Albuquerque and Van Rheede had failed. The Ruler of Travancore also was gifted with sufficient foresight to realise the dangerous character of the new portent. Besides Rama Varma was himself involved in frontier troubles with the Governor of the Subedar of Arcot at Madura. Yusuf Khan, a rebellious subordinate who had himself been sent from Trichinopoly to displace another rebellious Sirdar, attacked Kalacaud in the territory of Travancore and took possession of it. The attitude of the Nawab of Carnatic was also doubtful as he was in correspondence with the Zamorin and encouraging him to continue the war with Travancore. A treaty was therefore negotiated by which the Zamorin agreed to pay Rs. 15,99,99 as indemnity and to withdraw from the Cochin territory.

This was the last war between Cochin and Calicut. In the same year as this treaty was signed, 1762, Hyder Ali had attacked and conquered Mangalore,

Bednore and other important points on the West Coast immediately to the north of Malabar. The Mysore storm broke over the whole of Northern Kerala within the next few years sweeping away before its advance the military power of the Nayars and the political institutions of Kerala. With the treaty of 1762, the last page in the independent history of Kerala may be said to have been written. With this date the Nayar hegemony of Malabar may be said to end. So far the history of Malabar had been the history of the Nayars. But in 1762, the military power of the Nayars is broken finally in Travancore and in Cochin, and within a few years it was completely wiped out in North Kerala.

The position which existed up to this time may be described in the following words of Logan, the distinguished historian of Malabar.[1] "I would," says he, "call attention to the central point of interest . . . . . in any descriptive and historical account of the Malayali race—the position, namely, which was occupied for centuries on centuries by the Nayar caste in the Civil and Military organization of the province—a position so unique and so lasting that but for foreign intervention there seems no reason why it should not have endured for centuries to come. Their functions in the body politic have been wisely described in their own traditions as "the eye", "the hand" and "the order" and to the present day we find them spread throughout the length and breadth of the land, but no longer—I could almost say alas!—"preventing the rights (of all classes) from being curtailed or suffered to fall into disuse."

1) Logan—Malabar, Vol. I, 1887, Preface III and IV.

The bulwark against the tyranny and oppression of their own rulers secured for the country a high state of happiness."

Alas! that hegemony which looked so secure was finally broken.

The expansion of Travancore was the first direct blow to the Nayar predominance. The Travancore state was founded as a military autocracy on the ruin of Nayar power. The instruments by which Martanda Varma annihilated the Nayar nobility of his state and conquered the Nayar kingdoms to the north of his state were essentially foreign. It was with foreign mercenaries that he expanded his territory and it was with an essentially Tamilian bureaucracy that he governed it. Martanda Varma never forgot—and his successors have cherished the tradition—the troubles that the Ettuveetil chiefs had given to his house for over three centuries and in the new State that he founded he took good care to see that the Nayar nobility had no position and no power. In the home provinces of the Rajahs of Travancore the Nayar nobility had been systematically annihilated. In the conquered areas the ruling families were reduced to poverty and their nobles soon discovered that power and prestige no longer belonged to them. It was a purely bureaucratic state that Martanda Varma founded and his officials were mainly recruited from the small Tamilian minority in the South. The dominion of petty Malabar sovereigns and princes had come to an end, as Fra Bartolomeo observed at the time.

The example of the ruler of Travancore and the

success which attended the dispossession of the Nobles and their exclusion from political authority were not lost on the Prime Minister of Cochin. The chief of Paliyam, Komu Menon, who was instrumental in negotiating treaty with Travancore, had learnt state-craft in the school of Martanda Varma. After the success of the campaign against the Zamorin, Komu Menon took in hand the problem of organising the State of Cochin on the model of Travancore. Cochin as we had occasion to point out was never really a State. The Rajah's territorial authority was confined to a very small area while even the districts lying adjacent to his palaces and temples were in the hands of Nayar chiefs. This was one of the chief causes of the weakness of Cochin as these chiefs often changed sides and supported the Zamorin. Komu Menon realized that if Cochin was to be organized into a state the reduction of the power and territorial influence of these feudal barons was necessary. With the object in view, Komu Menon had inserted a clause in the treaty with Travancore that the Travancore Rajah will help the authorities in Cochin in their efforts to reduce the power of the nobles. As soon as the war was over the leading noblemen like Mankata Rajah, Chengazhi Nambiar and others who had helped the Zamorin were brought before the Rajah and made to realize that the days of political power were gone for them. Komu Menon proceeded also to confiscate and disinherit many minor noble families who had taken arms against the Rajah. By systematically enforcing this policy over a period of three years Komu Menon was able to establish the Rajah's power in Cochin on a sound and stable basis. But here also the establishment of the bureaucratic state meant the destruction of Nayar power. But it took a different form. The Nayar nobility disappeared from Cochin history. No more do we hear of Anchikaimals, Kodassery Kartavus and Chengazhi Nambiars. But the bureaucratic machinery was predominantly Nayar and therefore in the place of the baronial families there arose a new class of Nayar officialdom dependent on the pleasure, and upholding the power, of the Rajah.

During these years between the treaty of Mavelikkara and the invasion of Malabar by Hyder Ali, the political power of the Dutch had practically ceased all over Malabar. In the course of the northern expansion of Travancore, all that the Dutch commandeurs asked was that their immediate possessions should not be attacked. Martanda Varma annexed Karappuram over which they had definite and well established rights and they were unable to protest. His successor annexed Mangat and Parur, two states in whose affairs the Company had long interfered even to the extent of forcing the Rajahs to accept its unquestioned suzerainty. The Dutch were powerless to intervene even in this. The glory of Van Goens, Van Rheede and Van Imhoff had departed and the Dutch flag flew over Cochin merely on sufferance.

CHAPTER VIII

THE DISAPPEARANCE OF THE DUTCH

It is not proposed in this book to narrate in detail the story of the Mysorean invasion of Malabar. The subject is alluded only to complete the history of the Dutch settlement on the coast. In 1766 Hyder Ali made himself master of the kingdom of Chirakkal. In the same year he took Calicut, the Zamorin committing suicide by setting fire to the palace. The Dutch were alarmed at these unexpected developments and were afraid that Hyder might turn his attention towards them. With a view to placate him, Breekpot who was the commandeur of Cochin sent his commissioners to Calicut with presents to compliment Hyder on his success and to find out what his attitude was towards them. The Dutch submitted that their rights in Mapranam and Chetwai should be respected and that the Rajahs of Travancore and Cochin as the allies of the Company should not be attacked. Hyder received these proposals and in his turn suggested a trade agreement on the following conditions:

1. That the Company should enter into an offensive and defensive alliance with him.
2. That in his southern campaigns the Company should provide him with 1000 European soldiers.

3. That he was prepared to respect the Company's rights in Chetwai and Mapranam subject to his right to march through them.

He agreed to spare the Rajahs of Cochin and Travancore provided Cochin paid him an annual tribute of 4 lacs and eight elephants and Travancore 15 lacs and 30 elephants. The commandeur was not in a position to accept these extensive commitments and therefore he replied that the matter would have to be referred to Batavia. The Company, however, communicated the terms to the Rajah of Travancore whose reply to this humiliating proposal was the erection of defence works on the northern boundary of the State up to Cranganore.

The dilatory reply of the Dutch met the situation for the time as Hyder was called away from Malabar by the news of the Maratha invasion. In 1773 he again turned his attention to Malabar. He annexed the territory of the Zamorin and placed it under his own officers. The Mysorean Governor at Calicut immediately began to press the claims which his master had inherited from the Zamorin. The principality of Cranganore was formerly subject to Calicut and the Mysorean general lost no time in demanding that the Rajah should pay a tribute and accept his authority. Moens who had become commandeur of Cochin in 1771 claimed that Cranganore was a fief of the Company and tried to intervene in order to save that principality from Mysorean attack. But Sirdar Khan, Hyder's general, refused to listen to the expostulations of the Dutch and the Rajah was forced to yield.

In 1776 Hyder demanded of the Dutch free passage to attack Travancore. Moens replied that no answer had come from Batavia. Hyder knew that this reply was dishonest because it was over 10 years since he made that condition which Breekpot had referred to Batavia. Furious at this double dealing of the Dutch Sirdar Khan invaded Cochin territory marching through areas over which the Dutch claimed rights. In August 1776 Sirdar Khan captured Trichur. The Company could do nothing to protect its ally and vassal and in its anxiety to retain the trade looked on unconcerned while the Rajah of Cochin was being humiliated.

Now it was their turn. Chetwai was formerly a portion of the Zamorin's territory and Sirdar Khan now claimed accounts and arrears for the administration of that area. The Company did not know what to do. They had tried to placate Hyder, had sent him presents and had allowed the Rajahs of Cochin and Cranganore to be despoiled. The position of the Company was humiliating but as the Dutch were unable to oppose Hyder by force of arms, they sent him an account which showed that the Zamorin was in arrears. Without waiting for further correspondence the Khan crossed the river a little to the south of Chetwai and took the Dutch officials prisoners and demanded the payment of 20 years' revenue. From thence the General invaded Pappanetty and after having reduced it and taken up his headquarters at the Dutch Residency, he wrote to the commandeur complaining that he had not received any reply to his letters. He then invaded Cranganore and laid siege to the Company's fortress there.

The Company had by this lost all its territorial possessions. Chetwai and Pappanetty passed to Hyder without the Company striking a blow in its defence and Cranganore was also reduced. Besides this, the Khan also demanded 20 years' revenue for the lands of the Zamorin which the Company had held. Now there was no option for the Company. They had either to abdicate and withdraw with ignominy or resist Hyder's demands by force. Moens approached the Rajahs of Travancore and Cochin with a proposal that they should ally themselves with him to resist Hyder. It was clear that what the Mysore King wanted was to reduce Travancore. Moens had therefore some hopes that the Ruler of Travancore would declare himself openly for an alliance. But Rama Varma knew that the Dutch in Cochin had not sufficient strength to be of any help to him and replied that as he had allied himself with the English and the Nawab of the Carnatic he could only act in concert with them. So he declined the alliance adding, however, that he would be willing to concert defensive measures.

Thus thrown back upon their own strength the Company asked the Colombo Government to send them reinforcements immediately. Aya Kotta was fortified and proper defensive arrangements were undertaken. It was feared that the Mysoreans would attack Cranganore from the sea. On the arrival of the reinforcements for the Dutch, the Mysorean did not open the attack on Aya Kotta.

Moens, satisfied that his honour had been saved, was now anxious to open negotiations with Hyder. A letter which had arrived from the Supreme Government at Batavia was, therefore, despatched to Seringapatam with suitable presents. In reply Hyder stated that he had only feelings of friendliness towards the Dutch and was willing to enter into an alliance with them. To this the commandeur sent an evasive reply. He pretended anxiety to be on friendly terms but was actually planning to recover what the Company had lost to Hyder. An expedition was sent to Cranganore early in 1778 which re-occupied that principality and attacked Pappanetty. The expedition advanced so far as Chetwai but there it met the Mysore forces and suffered a heavy defeat, entailing the loss of some guns. The Dutch troops retreated to Cranganore with their morale badly shaken. Fortunately for the Dutch war broke out between the English and Hyder which prevented him from actively pursuing his schemes in Malabar.

For the rest of Hyder's life-time the Dutch were safe. But Tipu who succeeded his father in 1782 was not inclined to give up the claims which Hyder had pegged out in Malabar. In 1788 Tipu proposed to the Dutch commandeur at Cochin an offensive and defensive alliance. But the Dutch as usual were cautious and nothing came of the proposal. Then he proposed that the Company should sell him the fort of Cochin, Cranganore and Aya Kotta. The fortress at Aya Kotta was the main obstacle in his projected attack on Travancore lines. These lines had been constructed in

1764 by the Travancore Rajah on the advice of General de Lannoy. The Flemish soldier who had considerable engineering skill had noticed during his northern campaign in support of Cochin, how open the new boundary of Travancore was to any attack from the north. Therefore he designed a long and defensible line which is thus described by George Powney, the English East India Company's Agent at Trivandrum in a letter to the Governor of Madras dated 17th February 1790: "They run from West to East commencing at the sea on the island of Vaipin and continue to a broad river called Chinnamangalam on the opposite bank of which they begin again and extend to Annimally or Elephant mountains where they terminate on the top of one of them...... The lines consist of a ditch about 16 feet broad and 20 feet deep with a thick bamboo hedge in it a flight parapet and good rampart and bastions on rising grounds, almost flanking each other. From one extreme of the lines to the other they are only assailable by regular approaches from the north."

For the attack on these lines the possession of Aya Kotta fort was indispensable and it is with this object in view that Tipu offered to buy that fort from the Dutch. But the commandeur, instead of acceding to the request, immediately approached the Rajah of Travancore and by an agreement dated 31st July 1789 sold the forts of Cranganore and Cochin to him. The agreement reads as follows:

"The illustrious and mighty King of Travancore Wanjie Walla Martanda Rama Varmer having sent his first State Minister and Dalava his Excellency Krishna Poole to the Hon'ble John Gerard Van Anglebeck, Counsellor in ordinary of Netherlands India and Governor of the forts and possessions of the illustrious and mighty Netherlands East India Company on the coast of Malabar, to purchase from the said Company and receive over the fort of Cranganore and the outpost of Aya Kotta with the plantations and fields belonging thereto and they having agreed on the terms have concluded the sale on the following conditions.

The Dalava Krishna Poole for his master bought, and Governor Van Anglebeck has on account of the Company sold to the King of Travancore for the sum of three hundred thousand Surat silver rupees the fort of Cranganore and the outpost of Aya Kotta; with the cannon and thereto belonging ammunition as they at present are as also the powder but no firelocks, cartridges and other articles and moreover the following plantations and gardens—

The Musquito Island rented to Bellote duzepo Pailo for		300	Rupees.
The garden of Teilo Barky rented for		115	,,
Do.	Ascentio deRoza rented for	190	,,
Do.	Naga Shetty rented for	164	,,
Do.	Hendrick Mayer rented for	230	,,
Do.	Bappoo Probu rented for	64	,,
Do.	Allewyn rented for	810	,,

The garden of Dama Mussa
rented for 1220 Rupees.

Do. Arkell Iltopoe
rented for 119 „

Do. Tronotoe Barky
rented for 115 „

The purchase and sale is concluded with this condition that the King of Travancore shall not prevent the passage past the fort, either to boats belonging to Company, or to the King of Cochin and his subjects but all the same should they be empty or ladden with rice, paddy or goods of any denomination whatever, as also rafts of wood and bamboo etc., etc.; in a word all goods whatever without exception are to be allowed free, without molestation to pass and repass, and no new duties to be charged thereon.

The king promises expressly that the firewood, which must be brought from above Cranganore, shall not be prevented on any pretext whatever and no new charges laid thereon, but on the contrary will assist in forwarding the same to Cochin.

The Lepers' House at Palliport with its adjoining buildings, gardens and other grounds belonging thereto, is to remain in the Company's full and free possession.

The Roman Churches at Cranganore and Aya Kotta having for a long time been under the Company are to remain so and the King is not to trouble himself with them or the Priests; the Christians are to remain vassals of the Company and must not be burdened with any new taxes.

The Priests' House at Palliport, which the Governor

built and presented to the Church is to remain to the Church and no new taxes will be laid on them.

The inhabitants retain their houses, gardens and plantations which are now in their possession and as long as they remain Christians are like other Roman Catholic vassals of the Company, and must not therefore on any pretext whatever have any new taxes laid on them, but they are to be held answerable to pay unto the King whatever they formerly paid to the Company.

The king promises to pay a sum of fifty thousand rupees ready money, before the delivering over the above-mentioned forts and ground and the remainder being two hundred and fifty thousand rupees to be paid in the four next following years at equal periods and to be carried to the credit side of the pepper account yearly to the amount of sixty-two thousand five hundred rupees for the fulfilling of which for the merchants David Rahaboy, Ephrain Cohen and Anta Setty bind themselves as bonds-minor legal debtors. All this is agreed to in the city of Cochin in the year Koilang 974 the 19th of the month *Karkadagom* or the 31st July 1789."

For this piece of double dealing Tipu's wrath would have fallen on the Dutch but for the complications arising from his attack on Travancore and the third Mysore War which it precipitated. By the treaty of 1792 Tipu lost his Malabar possessions and the Dutch had nothing more to fear from him.

The possessions of the Dutch had already been reduced to the Cochin fort and a few acres near Quilon. With the conquest of Malabar by the British the position of the Dutch, as traders, suffered and Cochin ceased to be of any importance. But even as a relic of the days of Van Goens and Van Rheede they were not destined to hold it for long. The war between England and France caught Holland in its toil and the alliance of the Batavian republic with Revolutionary France gave the British Company an opportunity to demand the surrender of Cochin. To enforce this demand a force under Major Petrie marched down from Calicut. But the Dutch Governor Van Spall refused to yield. A force was therefore landed to the south of Cochin. This consisted, besides one regiment of European soldiers, of a battalion of sepoys, and a strong force of artillery. As soon as fire was opened Van Spall sent his proposals for surrender. Though many conditions were made Major Petrie refused to agree and the commandeur rather ingloriously accepted the terms offered to him. Major Petrie agreed to give the garrison the honours of war. The officers were allowed to retain their swords. The garrison marched out in military formation and deposited their arms upon the esplanade and returned as prisoners of war. The request that they should be repatriated was refused by Major Petrie who bluntly stated that the garrison will be disposed of as the commander-in-chief may direct. With this, the Dutch flag ceased to fly on the Malabar coast (20th October 1795). The formal cession took place by the Convention of Paris in 1814 when the alliance with Revolutionary France which had been so disastrous to the Colonial Empire of Holland, was broken by the defeat of Napoleon.

CHAPTER IX

DUTCH POLICY IN MALABAR

The Dutch policy in Malabar was governed by the single consideration of maximum pepper trade at minimum expense. The original idea with which the Dutch started was a monopoly in pepper trade by agreements with the Chieftains and Rajahs whose territories lay to the south of the Zamorin's kingdom. These contracts, which were negotiated with the Princes immediately after the conquest of Cochin, all contained a clause that pepper should be sold only to the Dutch Company. Such an agreement was clearly difficult to enforce without political power backed by a considerable army. That was, indeed, what was attempted until the rise of Martanda Varma and the treaty of Mavelikkarai which crushed the political authority of the Company.

The policy of the Company falls distinctly into 3 periods: (1) from 1664 to 1697, (2) from 1697-1717 and (3) 1717-1754. During the first period the Company maintained a considerable military establishment and kept up the pretence of great power. The attempt at that time was to enforce rigorously the pepper contracts with the rulers. The authorities embarked on a forward policy in Cochin and reduced the Rajah of that place to utter dependence. They claimed the right to interfere in every matter concerning the administration of the State and even in the internal affairs of the

Royal family. Nor were their pretensions any less in Cranganore whose Chief was declared to be a bondsman of the Company. At other places where the seat of the Ruler was not within the range of the Company's guns their claims were not taken seriously. But in the lands of the petty lords round about Cochin, in Mangat, Parur and Idappalli they interfered, claimed and enforced political control.

This policy was found to entail vast expenditure on military establishments. If the authority of the Company was to be felt and feared military posts all over the coast could not be avoided and this would naturally lead to incessant trouble. Defiant Chieftains would have to be punished. The military posts must always be in a satisfactory condition for defence against local inhabitants. In spite of these the major princes may take no heed. This is exactly what happened. Though the Company's military establishment cost a great deal, it produced no satisfactory results. The monopoly in pepper trade could not be enforced. The Rajahs were openly selling to outsiders, and the Chief of Kayamkulam, in whose territory there was a military post of importance, was harbouring Captain Kydd and selling pepper to him.[1] The failure of the policy of enforcing by arms the pepper contracts was so clear that in 1697 the Company decided to reduce the garrison and withdraw from a number of outposts it had built. The Resolution said:

1. "That the fortifications of the city of Cochin, which by the large garrison it required and the

1) Zvaadekroon's Memorial, 31st May 1698.

continual reparations to be made in consequence of the great extent of the walls were too expensive for the Company to maintain, should be reduced by one-half.

2. That one of the present fortifications of Cannanore, the Portuguese tower, only should be preserved with a garrison of 20 or at the most 25 Europeans.
3. That in Cranganore the ancient interior works should be preserved with a garrison of 20 Europeans which is judged a sufficient number for the purposes of the Company there.
4. That it is likewise judged advisable at Quilon no more should be retained than the old Portuguese tower or as much of the present works as may be thought necessary, for the interests of the Company with 15 or 20 men to which number the establishment should be reduced; and that the remainder of the fortification of the 3 last places should be removed or demolished.

It was further thereby determined that all military outposts should be withdrawn except Paponetty, Proca and Cali Coylang (Kayamkulam) should be maintained as residences or factors in order to keep an eye over what might be going forward all along the coast."[1]

Similar reductions were made in all naval and artillery establishments of the Company. The vessels were reduced to one small yacht, two sloops and three small row boats. In fact, the Company never attempted to

1) Stravoninus, Vol. III. p. 235.

enforce the Portuguese policy of completely restraining navigation and never claimed to be the sole lords of the seas. Such a claim was impossible as the English and French and other European nations were keen competitors on the Malabar Seas. Besides, the Dutch had a considerable fleet at Colombo which was always available for use in Malabar. Artillery on the coast was fixed at 95 pieces of iron, six pieces of brass, and ordnance with two motors.

This extensive reduction in the military establishment of the Company was undertaken because "the ostentation of a great power which cost the Company such large sums of money had not the effect of producing on the native princes that degree of awe and apprehension which is indispensably necessary for the carrying on of an extensive trade". But these retrenchments undertaken in the interests of larger profits did not help the affairs of the Company. Almost immediately after this, war broke out between the Company and the Zamorin which really came to a close only in 1717 after an extended campaign involving the use of a very large European army. In this period—between 1697 and 1717—the Company's policy was to reduce military establishments, but they were forced to carry on a defensive and later on an offensive war against the King of Calicut who was not included in their political system.

Even after the conclusion of peace with the Zamorin the charges grew to such an extent that the Supreme Government at Batavia issued strict injunction (by their secret despatches dated 30th September 1721) not to continue hostilities against the princes on the coast.

They went even to the extent of saying that the Company should not interfere to support the Rajah of Cochin if he were attacked by the Zamorin. After 1717, the policy of the Company, as we have traced elsewhere, was one of increasing intervention in the affairs of the smaller princes. The prestige which they had gained by the defeat of the Zamorin was of help in bringing the petty Chiefs under control. With the Madampies or petty chiefs of Karappuram they made a treaty at Aryat in 1710, but the policy of intervention in the internal affairs of the chiefs developed only after 1717. Gollenese even went to the extent[1] of suggesting that the principalities of Vadakkumkur and Parittally should be conquered and held directly by the Company. But of its feasibility he himself was not certain and his proposal was therefore couched in the following equivocal terms. "However should the Company have a great force at any time in India and occasion permit us to push the matter energetically my opinion would be that it would suffice to make ourselves completely master of the states of Peritally and Vadakkumkur." Van Imhoff who visited Malabar in 1739[2] was even more imperialistic and wanted the Company to "punish" the princes who were defiant.

The rise of Martanda Varma foiled their plans. Their whole policy of internal intervention and the claim to political power were given up by the treaty of Mavelikkara. The Company by the famous 9th Article of the treaty receded from all engagements

1) See Chapter III.

2) Madras Records, page 72.

with the Princes whom the Travancore Rajah chose to attack and agreed to interfere on no account in their disputes, nor in any respect to raise any objection to the enterprises of the King. After this, the only object of the Company was to trade peacefully and to keep whatever little power they had in Cochin and its environs.

An attempt has recently been made by an English writer to prove[1] that the Dutch were sovereigns in Malabar from the beginning and had seriously entertained the idea of conquering the country. There is indeed no basis for such a claim. It is true that the Dutch Company was accepted as one of the Malabar powers and in Cochin they had sovereign authority on the pretext of which they intervened in the affairs of the petty states on the coast. But the whole territory of the Zamorin was completely outside their influence; the Rajahs of Travancore even before the time of Martanda Varma were more friendly towards the English Company than towards the Dutch; while the princes in the interior never even had dealings with them. Even the more powerful coastal chiefs like the Rajah of Kayamkulam did not consider the Company to be anything like a superior power. The power of the Company was in fact confined to Cochin and to such small states like Mangat and Parur which could be bullied and intimidated from the Capital. They were in fact exactly like one of the minor chiefs in Malabar and never at any time were they "the Paramount power in Malabar" as Mr. Galletti pompously declares. An ambitious man unacquainted with Malabar conditions

1) Mr. Galletti's "Dutch in Malabar" p. 25.

like Van Imhoff may have thought it possible to conquer portions of Malabar, but the authorities in Batavia recognised after some experience that wars only serve "on the one hand to reveal the impotence of the Europeans against the Natives of the country if they have to be brought to reason by force of arms, on the other hand to impose a great and unbearable burden on us rather than to bring to the Company something substantial proportioned to the great hazards, inconveniences, burdens and crosses which it has brought on itself by the Wars."[1] Even Gollenesse when he suggested that Peritally and Vadakkumkur may be conquered did so in full realisation of its impossibility. The Dutch were never, and did not at any time attempt to be, the paramount power in Malabar. All that they claimed politically was authority over Cochin and its dependencies and at Quilon.

The Dutch policy in Malabar had to fight against the rivalry of other European nations all over the coast. The English had established a factory at Purakkad in 1664, from which they were sent away by the Rajah as a result of the agreement with the Dutch. The English were prepared to pay a higher price for pepper and buy it in the open market, and therefore their competition soon became very keen. The Dutch Policy from the beginning was directed towards a "blockade from the land" by prohibiting the Rajahs from selling pepper to the English. "Every means should be employed" wrote Their High Mightinesses in a letter dated Amsterdam, May 14th. 1667, "and

1) Moens p. 106.

every effort made to have the English expelled from the land of the Zamorin. The present time of war is a suitable occasion to achieve this. It will never do to have that nation settled so near us."[1] As the Zamorin could not be persuaded to expel the English, the Dutch attempted to prevent merchants from selling pepper to the English. This also was unsuccessful and was given up in 1669. "Although last year we prevented any pepper from reaching the English from Cannanore, we know that they have received large quantities. Therefore we need not trouble ourselves to buy pepper at Cannanore at such high prices for the sake of preventing other nations."[2]

In 1669 the Dutch and the French established themselves again in Calicut. The Zamorin was very friendly especially towards the English and helped them to attract to his port much of the pepper that was produced in Vadakkumkur and Thekkumkur. This competition rendered the pepper very dear for the Dutch and they attempted to intercept the land route by persuading the Rajah of Cochin to attack the chiefs through whose territory the trade was carried on.[3] In 1690 the English were established at Anjengo and diverted to that factory the pepper, cardamom and cloth trade of Travancore. The real competition between English and the Dutch began, however, only with the arrival of Robert Adams in 1716 as the Chief of the Calicut factory. Robert Adams

1) Dutch Records at the Hague—Letter dated May 14th 1607.

2) Letter Amsterdam, August 25th 1669.

3) Letter of November 17th 1669, from Governor-General, Vol. 29, D. CCC, p. 6.

was a masterful man and he soon became a great favourite of the Zamorin. As we have seen, he received from the Zamorin the right to establish a trading centre at Chetwai and in return helped that ruler greatly in the war against the Dutch. The English were thus well established at Tellicherry, Calicut and Anjengo, with the result that the Dutch had no prospect at any time of having the pepper monopoly or political predominance at Malabar. Naturally, they hated these intruders and did not fail to intrigue with the Rajahs to their detriment. But as they kept strictly aloof from political complications, their trade prospered while that of the Dutch declined.

Other European powers who had interests on the Malabar coast were the French and the Danes. The French were established at Mahe in 1725. The Danes had for sometime close relations with Calicut, for in 1756 the Dutch Commandeur complained about the Danes supplying the Zamorin with arms and ammunition.

Though, in the days of the monopolistic pretensions, the Dutch Company looked upon the European nations as intruders, with the decline of their political power and the increase in the stability of the English Company after the union of the two rival adventurers, the Dutch attitude towards them changed greatly. Though there was never any cordiality the Dutch ceased to look upon the English and the French as those who were unjustly interfering in their business. The English Company, in many ways more far-sighted, while keeping itself strictly outside political entanglements, was not loath to supply arms and ammunition to all those who fought against the Dutch. Thus the Zamorin in his various campaigns against Cochin, and Travancore in its prolonged and successful wars against the pretensions of Gollenesse and Van Imhoff were able to depend upon the English factory at Calicut and at Anjengo for an uninterrupted supply of arms and ammunition.

There is another point with regard to the Dutch policy in Malabar which is worth notice. Malabar was only an unimportant part of the Dutch settlements in the East. It was subordinate not only to the supreme government at Batavia but to the government of Ceylon. Naturally it was not able to pursue a forward policy and often its schemes could come to nothing for want of adequate support from Ceylon and Batavia.

The failure of the Dutch policy in Malabar was due to a variety of reasons. The first and the most important cause was the rise of Travancore as a powerful military state. The Company after its first effort to impose its will by the pretence of great military power had given up the idea in 1697. Their methods of action after that lay in working through the instrumentality of the Rajah of Cochin and the Christian population over whom they claimed special rights. They also asserted a right to maintain the balance of power in Malabar. The rise of Travancore demonstrated the hollowness of their military pretensions and destroyed the balance of power on which they depended for their trade. All the minor chieftains in whose affairs the Company had habitually interfered for over half a century, the Rajahs of Mangat, Parur, Vadakkumkur, Tekkumkur, Purakkad, Desinganad, Maruthurkulangara, Peritally and Attungal disappeared all of a sudden from the map and were absorbed into one single state. In the territories of the Zamorin the Company had no power at any time. In the territories of Travancore, extending to the very borders of the town of Cochin, the Company's power was destroyed by the growth of Travancore. Even the special right of jurisdiction over coastal Christians which the Company enjoyed at Quilon, which was a useful method of interfering in the affairs of states had to be given up.

The final and total disappearance of the Dutch from the mainland as from Ceylon was due to a cause over which they had no control—the rise of the British power in India. In 1795, when Cochin was taken away from them, the British had already become one of the leading powers in India. The fight with England, as a result of the Napoleonic wars cost Holland much besides the little settlement in Cochin. Otherwise it might have continued as a picturesque survival like Mahe, Daman, or Chandernagore. Its political importance was lost in 1758 but it disappeared as Dutch possession only 40 years later.

A second cause of the failure of the Company's policy was the presence of other European nations whose commercial interests were opposed to those of the Company. This position helped the states to organise opposition on effective lines. The armies of the rulers had improved a great deal since the time of Vasco da Gama, and the Companies which de Lannoy trained for Martanda Varma were in no way inferior to the soldiers whom the Dutch were able to put in the field. Their supply of arms and ammunition was guaranteed by the presence of the English and the French on the coast and the Dutch could not in the 18th century compete with either of these nations for naval supremacy. The Dutch position on the coast was altogether untenable and the growth of Travancore power abolished it altogether.

What is important to note is that the destruction of Dutch power in Malabar was in no way due to the inefficiency of the Company or to the disorganisation of the Company's administration. Their officers from Hutstaart to Moens were with few exceptions men trained in administration and highly competent both in business and in government. The system of councils and superintendence by commissaries sent out from headquarters kept the administrative machinery always in good form. Every action was duly deliberated upon, communicated in writing to superior authorities, who kept a watchful eye on all proceedings. The system of letters to the supreme government at Batavia was extremely useful because every step taken had to be defended to a body which was closely in touch with administrative details. It was a bureaucratic system, and it had all the virtues of bureaucracy without its disadvantages. As the business of the Company was mainly commercial, its strict methods of work, which reduced it to a soulless machinery did not have the evil, which is inherent in bureaucratic government, of divorcing the officials from the people.

Unlike the Portuguese again, the Dutch Company was never in difficulties about its finance. The Company was primarily a trading corporation and never for a moment were its officers allowed to forget that important fact. Any undertaking which involved unnecessary expense was ruthlessly vetoed whatever other benefits might follow from it. The accounts were kept with scrupulous care, pay was never in arrears, and the economical management of all establishments was insisted upon by the authorities. All these present a most striking contrast to the affairs of the Portuguese in India which was always on the verge of bankruptcy owing to inefficiency of its financial administrators. So far as the Dutch were concerned, their superiority over all the other powers, Indian as well as European, was amply clear from the very beginning. That is what made their settlements in Malabar prosperous even when their political authority had disappeared. It was a standing order of the Government that every retiring chief should leave a memorandum on the state of Malabar for his successor. This was an exceptionally good plan as it ensured continuity of policy and provided a source of authoritative information for successive administrators. As Moens points out in the preface to his memoir "the affairs of Malabar are so inextricably bound up and mutually connected that if you would wish at the outset of your administration to meddle with an affair of little importance (no matter what good object you may have in view) it may sometime or other cause a derangement which on account of your not being acquainted with the particulars, could not have been anticipated." This useful system prevented the Dutch from falling into many of the grave errors into which successive Portuguese captains of Cochin fell through their ignorance.

The Dutch connection with Malabar was not marred by massacres, and other acts of inhuman cruelty which characterised the Portuguese. The only occasion in which the Dutch soldiers desecrated a temple was in the case of a pagoda belonging to the Punnathur Nambidi—in the war against the Zamorin. But even this outrage was committed by Balinese soldiers against the orders of the Dutch commandeur. In their wars against Malabar rulers, they never set fire to towns, or felled fruit-bearing palms or took as captives women and children as the Portuguese did. The barbarities which the Portuguese captains perpetrated on the sea against the Moors were unheard of in the time of the Dutch. In fact, they prided, and with reason, on their humanity. When Captain Nieuhoff was asked by the Rajah of Travancore as to whether he would do less than the Portuguese did, he retorted, that if he wanted to imitate the Portuguese he would have to murder and pillage which was against the policy of the Company. As a result, the Dutch were never so unpopular on the coast as the Portuguese had been. Many of the Dutch captains were actually popular with the Malabar rulers with whom they maintained the most friendly intercourse.

The Dutch were staunch Protestants and their hatred of the Portuguese intensified their religious bigotry. But as a whole they were liberal and tolerant and after the first years of destructive zeal they did not interfere with the Catholics. But immediately on the conquest of Cochin, their religious zeal carried them to the extraordinary length of pulling down even the magnificent jesuit library. Tavernier narrates the incident thus: "You must know that at the taking of Cochin, the jesuits had in that city one of the fairest libraries in all Asia, as well as for the great quantity of books sent them out of Europe as for the several rare manuscripts, the Hebrew, Chaldaic, Arabic, Persian, Indian, Chinese and other oriental languages. During the little time that the jesuits were in Ethiopia they had copied out all the books that came into their knowledge and sent all these books to Cochin. But to tell of what became of this library, General Van Goens made no convenience to expose it to the ignorance of his soldiers, so that I have seen soldiers and seamen tear several of these beautiful volumes to light their tobacco."[1] Their vandalism in pulling down the sacred edifices has already been mentioned. Even Canter Visscher says "This town formerly contained handsome churches but they have either been demolished or converted into magazines."

After their first zeal was over the Dutch followed a liberal policy towards the Catholics. The jesuits who had to leave when the Dutch conquered Cochin

1) Quoted in Whitehouse Beginnings of Light in a Dark land, Page 132. Madras Records 13.

were allowed to come back. They were allowed freedom to govern the diocese and were "even permitted to settle down within the territories of the Company, to be precise, at Ambalakkad, a village 3 hours beyond Cranganore." At this place the jesuits had a college where free instruction was given. In 1676, 3 Carmelite fathers obtained permission to come to Cochin. The purpose of their visit was to appoint a coadjutor in place of Alexander de Campo who was greatly advanced in age. They had instruction to appoint someone to whom the Company had no objection. The Company did not desire to have Portuguese Bishops resident in Cochin and therefore chose Mathias de Campo. But this was not acceptable to Rome. The relations between the Dutch commandeurs and the Roman Bishops continued, however, to be cordial.

The Roman Catholics in Cochin and in Quilon were specially under the protection of the Company. In this matter the Dutch continued the policy of the Portuguese and utilised the privileges of the Catholics for the increase of the political power of the Company. They were, as noticed before, under the jurisdiction of the Company's officers. But as the strict operation of the clause would have meant immunity for the Latin Catholics living inland a later treaty (1664) stipulated that those remaining inland should obey the Rajah's government.

The Latin Catholics who were subject to Cochin were not slow to take advantage of these privileges. They defied the Rajah's government and depended on the Company for protection. They evaded the Rajah's taxes. The explanation that Governor Moens gives in his *memorial* is this. "As the Christians (paraya converts) are much despised by the heathens they should have to suffer humiliation and would be ill-treated if they were not protected by the Company". The commandeur did not limit his intervention in the case of Christians who were badly treated. He interfered in order to maintain the rights of free worship. "Besides the above," says Moens, "the Christian subjects (meaning the new Catholics) have the privilege that they only pay half the taxes to the king". It was natural that this right should give rise to constant disputes. The Company claimed that they had jurisdiction over all Catholics while the Rajah insisted that the treaty of 1664 gave them right only over the converted fishermen of the coast. Gradually as the authority of the Company diminished the Rajah's rights over these Christians increased.

The friendly policy of the Protestant Company towards the Catholics was much appreciated at Rome. Pope Clement XIV conveyed his thanks in a special *Brief* which he addressed to the vicar apostolic of Malabar in the following terms:—

"Greetings to Our Reverend Brother; our beloved Son, Stephen Boyd secretary to the congregation for the propagation of Christians has communicated to us in detail the attention paid and the trouble taken by the Dutch Governor for the safety of the Christians who are there yonder. And as such Christian acts of kindness undoubtedly concern us greatly, and as on their account, we are indebted to him, so it is our earnest desire that least our feelings of gratitude for the same be made known and clear to his man. Therefore, to show our gratitude we have hereby to recommend to your reverence, to assure him of our grateful sentiments in the most forcible and the most striking manner and at the same time to testify that we feel ourselves so much more indebted to him for what he has done as we flatter ourselves that he will continue in this way to lay the Christians and us under further obligation."

Given at Rome the 23rd July 1772 in the 4th year of our papal reign: Stephen Borgia.

The Company treated the Roman Bishops with much ceremony. The Bishop of Verapoly on arriving at the settlement when Moens arrived "was fetched by two councillors in a carriage and taken to the residence of the Chief where the so called[1] bodyguard was lined up under the command of an officer and as the Bishop passed, both this and the main guard presented arms and made the salute with the spontoon. As he ascended the steps a salute of nine guns was fired from the walls of the town."

The Dutch had originally ideas about converting the low[2] class Catholics of the coast to their own religion. But Gollenesse confesses 'to his sincere regret' that "the Reformed Doctrine has made little progress in spite of all careful forethought and regulations concerning schools and education of children and

1) Moens p. 157
2) Gollenesse Memoir p. 80.

instructions regarding the penetration of popish superstitions". The Dutch always maintained an ecclesiastical establishment, but they do not seem to have been able to influence the Catholic population into their ways of thought.

So far as the Syrian Christians were concerned the Company had no authority but the Commandeurs gave them steady support in their fight against Rome. As Moens says "we have after the conquest of Cochin not only favoured the revolt of the Eastern Christians against the usurpations of Rome but also assisted them in getting out new Bishops from Syria, by placing at their disposal the ships of the Company. The administrators of this coast and the preachers of the reformed community have not only kept up a correspondence with St. Thomas Christians about maintaining . . . the rights of the Eastern churches against the Bishops of the Roman Catholics, but have also displayed much zeal in attempting to unite them with the Protestant church."[1]

Towards the Hindus the Dutch policy was tolerant and liberal. Unlike the Portuguese the Dutch were not consumed with a desire to convert the heathen. The Dutch uniformly respected the scruples of the Hindus. In a treaty with the Vadakkumkur Rajah, signed on the 29th September 1740, they undertook "not to molest Pagodas or cows." They went even so far as to insist on the due performance of Hindu ceremonies. The Company once demanded that certain Nampudiris should appear before the Comman-

1) Moens, p. 180.

deur and explain their worshipping at the pagoda of Chembukovil which was against ancient usage.

From all that has been said, it is clear that the Dutch on the Malabar coast formed in many ways a tolerant and civilising influence and their policy, in trade, administration as well as religion was based on sound and liberal ideas. They had no desire to exploit the people who came into contact with them, or to oppress them. Their one object was to carry on trade in such a way as to yield the largest amount of profits and ideas of glory, and desire for heavenly merit by converting the heathen and plundering his temples never entered into their calculations. Their intentions were friendly and the hundred years of their connection with Malabar constituted a period which was in many ways beneficial to the growth of civilisation in Malabar.

CHAPTER X

DUTCH ADMINISTRATION AND TRADE

(I) ADMINISTRATION

Unlike the Portuguese, the Dutch had from the very beginning an elaborate and highly efficient administrative system. They transplanted their own democratic organisation, developed at home, into their settlements in the East and even the smallest factory had its councils, committees and courts. The Portuguese administration was more or less a feudal system. It knew no discipline. The king and the high officials in Portugal interfered even in the minor details of administration, and every Portuguese factor in India had the right of direct communication with the court at Lisbon. The Dutch method differed from this. The "Dutch methods" were so superior to the Colonial systems then in vogue that it was the ambition of the English Company to copy them and to develop a system as much like the Dutch Government in the Indies as possible.

The Dutch Company was governed by a body of 17 directors, elected from among the principal bodies interested in the East India trade. These bodies were organised into Chambers which were autonomous in matter of accounts, internal government, etc. But the government of the settlements was a matter for the 17 directors, who through their sub-committees carried on the correspondence, issued directions and generally administered the affairs of the Company.

The settlements in the East were governed by a Governor-General in Council whose capital was at Batavia. The Council or their High Nobilities, as they were called, consisted of 9 members, four of whom were Governors of the outlying settlements. The head of the Administration was the Governor-General; but next to him in importance and in authority was the Director-General who was the head of the commercial affairs of the Company. The Council represented the different interests of the Company and was practically independent of the authority of their principals in Amsterdam.

Malabar was governed by the Commandeur and Council of Cochin. In the beginning there were five main outstations: Quilon, Kayamkulam, Purakkad, Cannanore and Cranganore. Thengapattanam was a residency. They were under Captains but their military force was reduced to a minimum. The Council of the Commandeur consisted of members of his political department and the Chief Military Officer on the coast. The number varied, but up to 1741 it was generally 9. The Chief Administrator who was the second in command was in special charge of the commercial affairs of the Company.

The service of the Company was divided into political, ecclesiastical and military. As the purpose of the political administration was commercial, the functions of the political officials included those of trade. At the head of the political service stood the Governor or Commandeur, and in minor stations, Resident or Captain. Below them was a heirarchy of officials from apprentice to upper merchant. The pay of the officials was not large. A Governor received 200 gilders while a Commandeur received only 150-180. But this was only the nominal pay. The officials were allowed commissions and perquisites which made the Governorships of Malabar a lucrative appointment. Article III of the Regulations declared that the Governors and Directors, and seconds in governments, directorships or commanderies, but no inferior chiefs or servants, shall be allowed to take what they want for their own use out of the company's warehouse upon paying 50 per cent. advance upon European and 30 per cent. upon Indian commodities, spices excepted. The Commandant of Malabar was to have one per cent. upon all goods imported and exported by private persons to be reckoned upon the sales of the former and the invoices of the latter. The Commandeur and the second in command were also permitted private trade. At the time of Moens this privilege was compounded and the Commandeur and his second received 5 per cent. on sales of merchandise and 3 per cent. on pepper bought. Of this sum the Commandeur was to get four-fifths and the second one-fifth.

The military establishment in Malabar was very small. It generally consisted of a Captain, one captain lieutenant, four lieutenants and six ensigns, 4 officers for Indian troops and 3 officers for artillery. The actual strength of the military force in peace time never exceeded 2000 of whom less than a half were Europeans. At the time of the war with the Zamorin and later on with the Travancore Rajah large reinforcements were brought from Colombo and Batavia, but generally speaking the military strength of the Dutch was negligible. The naval strength was no greater and it bore no comparison to the large squadrons which the Portuguese always had on the Malabar coast. At Cochin there was a Maritime officer but his squadron consisted only of one small yacht, two sloops and three row boats. A large Malabar squadron was not necessary for the Dutch for, from the first, they had decided[1] "not to obstruct any more by measures of constraint and harshness the navigation of the Malabars and their trade in the productions of their country". Besides the Dutch had a naval base at Colombo from where they could, if necessary, control the Indian seas.

Besides these essential organisations, the Dutch in Malabar had also many subsidiary institutions meant to secure the welfare of their factors. They had an excellent medical service, a fairly large number of skilled European workmen, for the repair of arms, for employment in the ship yards, etc.

The administration of Justice was a matter in which the Dutch took special pride. The *Memorial* of Moens gives a description of the courts, from which we could see the workings of the Dutch Judiciary in India.

"The Court of Justice here," says Moens, "consists of the Second in Council and Chief Administrator as President with most of the members of the political

1) Stravonines, Vol. III, p. 237.

Council and some other members of the services as members; which court as everywhere in India (i. e. Dutch Indies) decides and grants executions both in criminal and civil matters in the name and on behalf of Their High Mightinesses.

We have here a subordinate court also named the civil court or the court of small causes consisting of one of the members of the political Council here as president and some officers of inferior standing as members."

In the Commission given to Governors, Directors and Commandeurs it is among other things specially ordered that care should be taken that right and justice be administered among the people both in criminal and in civil cases. The Chiefs of Settlements used to preside in Courts of Justice as well as in the political councils but this naturally led to miscarriage of justice and to corruption. The evils of this system came prominently before Their High Mightinesses in the case of Peter Veeyst who utilised his position as Governor of Ceylon and Chief Justice of the Court to personal ends leading to the judicial murder of innocent people. This Governor, it must be said to the credit of the Dutch, was tried and publicly executed at Batavia in 1732. After this scandal the Second in Council in each settlement was given the presidency of the Courts of Justice.[1]

Moens complains that there were but few men in the Eastern settlements who had studied law. There

[1] P. 243 Selections from the Records of the Madras Govt., Dutch Records No. 13.

was no proper system of pleading and advocacy in courts. The Government lawyer (the advocate fiscal) had to plead both pro and contra and as Moens points out every "Fiscal is not of a sufficiently well balanced temperament to plead the cause of the accused with the same zeal as he employs to substantiate his own cause".

In criminal cases there were two kinds of procedure, the extraordinary, where strict proof was not required and ordinary cases where the rules of evidence and procedure were rigidly adhered to. The criminal cases affected the people of the country more than Europeans but the proceedings were entirely in Dutch and were conducted with the help of interpreters. Moens had an idea of training a number of Dutch people as interpreters. In fact he apprenticed Gerrit Van Waardenburg and Jacob Goliath to the second interpreter at Cochin for the purpose of learning Malayalam.

The company administered justice over the low caste Christians of the coast. By the treaty of 1663 it was specially laid down that the Christians "are under the jurisdiction of the company and if they committed a crime are punished only by the company. The company also exercised an appellate jurisdiction in cases affecting the Konkanis. The Konkanis were nominally under the Rajah of Cochin but they had the right of complaining against the Rajah to the company. "It is necessary," says Moens, "every now and then to make good our claim to the supreme authority reserved to us over them." As the Konkanis have most of their dealings with the people of the State this was a great encroachment on the judicial authority of the Rajah.

(II) TRADE AND REVENUE

The commercial policy of the Dutch differed from that of the Portuguese in many important respects. The circumstances of European trade had so considerably changed in the period between the 16th and the 18th century that the policy of complete monopoly which the Portuguese followed with success had been rendered impossible. The English and the French were established on the coast and carried away a great deal of the Malabar trade. At Tellicherry and Calicut the English established their position at the same time as the Dutch established themselves in Cochin. In Anjengo they built a factory in 1690 diverting into that factory most of the trade in the area south of Quilon. In 1725 a French squadron, which carried as one of its junior officers a young man by the name of Mahe' deLabourdannais, appeared on the Malabar coast and established a factory. Thus the advantage which the Portuguese had in being the sole European naval power on the Indian waters was denied to the Dutch from the very beginning. They had therefore to adjust their policy on the basis of this open competition.

The desire of the Dutch was to establish by contract with Indian rulers a monopoly in the goods they wanted to buy. In the agreements that Nieuhoff made with the Rajahs south of Cochin a clause was invariably inserted that "Nobody without any exception shall be permitted to export any pepper or cinnamon out of this country or sell it to anybody except the said company". With all Malabar Kings, except the Zamorin and the Rajah of Chirakkal, the Dutch had these agreements. The Rajahs accustomed to and accepting the Portuguese idea of monopoly did not demur at the demand of the Dutch. But they soon found that there were others who were prepared to buy their products at a higher price and despite agreements and treaties a considerable portion of pepper trade began to flow into other channels. The Dutch stigmatised the selling of pepper to other nations as contraband trade, and they attempted at first to put it down by force. But such a policy would have involved heavy expenditure, for which the Batavian authorities were not prepared, and military resources which they could ill spare. As Stravonines himself says "these attempts (to put down forcibly contraband trade) were as little productive of the effects proposed as they were expensive; for the princes themselves were not able to restrain their subjects from carrying on this trade with other nations, by which they made double the advantage they did in selling us".[1]

As the Company found out that in the altered circumstances "the ostentation of great power had not the effect of producing on the native princes that degree of awe and apprehension which is indispensably necessary for the carrying on of an extensive trade", they reduced their forces which further encouraged the

1) Stravonines Vol. III, p. 272.
Also see—'Secret considerations' De Jong—25th October 1757.

princes in their policy of defiance. In 1698, Zwaadekroon in a memorial dated 31st May complained that the company was so little feared by even the Rajah of Kayamkulam that he was openly trading with the notorious pirate, William Kidd. From the beginning the Dutch made no attempt to insist like the Portuguese that all trade on Indian seas should be carried on only in vessels permitted by them. The seaborne trade was to be free and the Company gave every facility for navigation.

Thus the trade of Malabar was not so profitable to the Dutch as it had been to the Portuguese; and the charges were proportionately heavy. They had to conduct 3 wars with the Zamorin and one with Travancore, even before the arrival of Hyder Ali in Malabar. The most serious military effort that was made was against the Zamorin in 1717. But even after that the charges did not go down. With the new plans of conquests which ambitious commandeurs developed after the treaty of 1717, the military expenditure and charges increased. Though on the basis of this added prestige they were able for a time to maintain their monopoly of pepper trade, it again ceased to yield satisfactory returns when the campaign against Travancore developed; and the conquest by Martanda Varma of the petty chieftainships up to Cochin made direct trade impossible in those areas.

The company's trade in Malabar was divided into two departments; investments for Europe, i. e. goods bought in Malabar for sale in Europe, and goods sold in Malabar. The stock merchandise which the company sold in Malabar consisted of sugar, Japanese bar, copper, tin, lead, silk stuff, camphor, vermillion, quick-silver. The Dutch Company had also a monopoly for the sale of opium and great profits were realised from this because it was the custom to exchange this for pepper. But Zwaadekroon[1] discontinued this method of forcing opium upon people. It was fortunate for Malabar that the great demand for opium in Java did not permit the Dutch to flood Malabar with it and after 1700, the sale of opium though large was not of sufficient importance to be considered a big item in the trade of the Company.

Of all the goods bought by the Company from Malabar pepper was of course the most important. The breakdown of the monopoly in pepper trade led to competition and Zwaadekroon, when he was Commissary for Malabar, recommended that pepper should be sold by the Company at the comparatively low profit of 25. This would have made competition impossible, because others buying direct from the Malabar market would have had to pay a higher price than that which was secured to the Company by agreement and the trade would not have yielded a profit. But Their High Mightinesses in Amsterdam disapproved of this excellent proposal and the premium was raised to 50 per cent. in 1725 and later in 1733 to 100 per cent. This policy was on the face of it suicidal. When the company was selling pepper at twice the price it bought, their private competitors as well as the English and French companies found it possible

1) Selections from Madras records—Vol. XIII, p. 70.

to pay a higher price on the market and still realise a reasonable profit at a price below what was the official price of the Dutch Company. This meant the quantity which came into the warehouse of the Company decreased year by year. Gollenesse advised that the whole system should be given up and a system of conquest must be undertaken especially of Peritally and Vadakkumkur. But this as we have seen ended in miserable failure, the Company after a conflict with Travancore withdrawing from all its positions and yielding up its political authority to Martanda Varma.

The Company soon accommodated itself to the new conditions and began to collect according to agreements where such a course was possible or by paying the market price where it was necessary. The Travancore Rajah was bound by treaty to sell to the Dutch 150,000 lbs. of pepper at Rs. 65 per candy of 500 lbs. from his hereditary possessions and 100,000 lbs. from his newly acquired territories at Rs. 55. As the English paid the Rajah Rs. 80 per candy and the Danes at Colachel still higher rates, he never supplied the Dutch with the full quantity stipulated. Moens in fact[1] complains that the Company gets only whatever is left and in times of draught, etc., it gets but little. It should have been clear that such a policy was bound to fail, because if the Dutch had not the power to enforce their contracts the Malabar princes would naturally sell the produce to those who could pay the best price. Out of the 2000 candies which the Travan-

1) P. 113.

core Rajah had promised he supplied at an average only 73 candies!

When collection according to contract ceased to be regular the Company was like other private traders forced to buy on the open market. The Company paid as much as Rs. 100 per candy in the market and oftentimes 120 to 135 when buying from Indian vessels. Moens mentions that during his term of office he bought 764,667 lbs. from private traders.

Next to pepper the most important trade when the Company first established itself on the coast was in cotton cloth made in South Travancore. The fine cloth made in Eraniel and Kottar has been famous for many centuries and the Portuguese carried on a very flourishing trade in it. When the Dutch Company expelled the Portuguese from the coast, Captain Nieuhoff who was the Chief at Quilon observed that Kottar was a centre of great traffic. The Company bought the piece-goods from the traders through their agents. An effort was also made at the time of Commandeur Gollenesse 1734-1743 to establish chintz dye-works under the protection of the Company. The Commandeur secured the services of some expert dyers from the East coast and settled them near Cochin. The attempt was not a success and the industry died out. But the Kottar piece-goods continued to be a large and important item of trade and found a ready market in the other colonies.

Cardamom was always one of the chief products of Malabar. The Dutch Company traded in it a great deal at the beginning but in course of time its importance diminished as other competitors arose in the field. The best cardamom grows in North Malabar where the English and the French paid such heavy prices that after a short and unsuccessful competition the Dutch practically gave up the idea of trading in it. They attempted to secure only the grain produced near Cochin in the territories of Kodassery Kaimal and the Rajah of Punjar. With the Kaimal they quarrelled and the cardamom from that source ceased to be available. The Rajah of Punjar refused to enter into a contract unless the Company secured for him "a small piece of land called Condasider" belonging to the Kutal Manikyam Devaswam at Irinjalakuda.

Malabar indigo was much in demand but though the plant grew wild in the country, only so much was produced as was required by the people. The Dutch on finding that it was of a superior quality introduced scientific cultivation of the plant in Mangat and Anjekaimal. Seed was sent for from Surat at the time of Gollenesse who encouraged the local people to take up its cultivation. It was also introduced on an extensive scale in Vendurtty, Chetwai, Pappanetty and Cranganore.

The import trade of Malabar was also to a large extent in the hands of the Dutch Company. The main objects in which they traded were opium, sugar, coffee, Chinese silks, Japanese copper and arms and ammunition. The company either imported direct or bought from Indian merchants who traded with those ports. They purchased generally by exchange. The trade in opium for which the Dutch were anxious when they came to Malabar ceased to be of importance because it was found possible to sell the drug at much higher price in Java and the Archipelago than what it fetched in Malabar.

Besides the revenues derived from trade the Company directly administered, or farmed out, considerable areas and derived much revenue out of them.

The most important estate was that of Dharmoth Panikkar. This was part of the estates belonging to Dharmoth Panikkar's family which by the treaty of 1717 passed in full proprietory right to the Company. It was situated in the northern limits of Pappinivattam (Pappanetty) and consisted 437 paras of sowing land (about 50 acres) 63 pieces of garden land and 22 slaves. The Company generally leased out these lands. These were in possession of the Company only up to the time of Hyder Ali's invasion.[1]

The Pazhayan Chery Nairs in 1755 offered to give the Company 492½ gold fanams (Rs. 190) 523 parras of rice. In 1764 they raised it to Rs. 341.

The Dutch held besides this, land round about Cochin, containing, according to Moens' memorial[2] 42089 cocoanut trees in the fruit-bearing stage, 500 acres of paddy land and 19,716 salt pans. There were altogether 9 islets and 69 gardens. Considerable income was derived from this. Other sources of income consisted of tolls and duties and the export of slaves. Every ship other than Dutch entering the ports of Cochin, Quilon or Cranganore had to pay port

1) Moens p. 134
2) Moens p. 207.

dues but of this half went to the Rajahs of the place. The export of slaves was a profitable concern: and the revenues derived from tobacco and from the sale of arrack formed another item of importance.

Malabar was always an "expensive" settlement from the point of view of the Company. Not that the Dutch did not make large profits. Even without counting the profits of the pepper trade in Holland the actual trade carried on in Malabar showed considerable profit. But the Company was never satisfied with less than 100 per cent. profit. The profits in pepper, which was sold in Europe at four times its purchase price were enormous but the Company did not calculate it as Malabar trade. The difference between the factories in Malabar and those in Ceylon and Java was that the Malabar settlement involved considerable military expenditure. The Company was always at war with the Malabar princes and had within 100 years to fight at least 4 major campaigns. Prolonged warfare exhausted the financial resources of the Company and destroyed its prestige. In the intervals however the Company made handsome profits. In 1770—1771 the expenditure amounted to £ 208,570-17 sh. while the income was £ 325,687-17 sh. This state of uncertainty in the profits of the Company arising from the political conditions of Malabar caused the more conservative section of Dutch opinion in Holland to demand the evacuation of Malabar or at least the restriction of operations to the trade in pepper. But with the conquest of Northern Malabar by Hyder Ali and later on the fight between Travancore and Mysore even pepper trade lost its value to the Dutch, so that when they yielded up Cochin to the English, the trade and revenue of that port had ceased to count in the trade of India.

CHAPTER XI

MALABAR AT THE END OF THE 18TH CENTURY

From the conquest of Cochin in 1663 to the breakdown of Dutch power lies a century which in many ways is the most important in Malabar history. During the course of that hundred years the whole political character of Malabar underwent a change. From the time of Cheraman Perumal to Martanda Varma, the political face of Malabar had remained the same. The division into petty principalities was traditional and even the Zamorin at the height of his power had not interfered with that arrangement. When the Dutch conquered Cochin there were in existence four "Kings" and 46 petty chieftains. The kings were the Rajahs of Chirakkal, the Zamorin of Calicut the Rajahs of Cochin and Travancore. Between Cochin and Travancore lay the 70 madampies of Karappuram, the Rajahs of Idappalle, Vadakkumkur, Tekkumkur, Punjar, Purakkad, Kayamkulam, Maruthurkulangarai, Deshingand, Peritally, Attungal and Vadayattu Pillai. At the end of the period all these states had been conquered and, what was more, annexed to Travancore. There was nothing new in one state conquering another. But annexation was new and against all the traditional ideas of Malabar polity. But Martanda Varma cared nothing whatever for Malabar ideals and annexed his conquests and reduced the chiefs to absolute poverty. By 1763, the present political divisions were practically complete. Cochin and Travancore and the Zamorin territory (later on British Malabar) stood out as the three divisions and the rest had disappeared to make room for the three.

There is some destiny that has decided against the unification of Malabar. Twice there was such a possibility and at each time, some unexpected foreign intervention prevented the consummation of that ideal. In the 15th century the Zamorin's power was steadily growing towards the south and there was every possibility of a unification of Malabar under the rule of the Zamorin. But the appearance of Vasco-da-Gama shattered that dream to pieces and checked the advance of the Zamorin at the ford of Idappalli. The next occasion was when the Travancore army marched up to Cochin to attack the forces of Calicut. But before Martanda Varma's dream of a united Malabar could be realised a new eruption, this time from the Mysore side, dashed the cup to pieces and divided Malabar for ever into three political divisions.

But the annexation of the smaller states and the division of Malabar into three kingdoms instead of thirty had two important results. It crushed the power of the Nayar nobility; and the feudal anarchy that reigned from one end of Malabar to another vanished never to return. Secondly, it marked the growth of Royal power and of the modern centralised bureaucratic state. Travancore, as we noticed before, was transformed by Martanda Varma into a military state based on a standing army and governed by a civil service which had but little to do with the people. The Nayar nobility had no voice in the administration and the Rajah's officials whose powers had enormously increased were recruited either from Tamilians of low birth and no standing or from among Nayars who were in no way connected with the old noble families. It is true that for sometime to come the administration, especially in the outlying districts was crude and inefficient. But that did not in any way affect the military character of the state or its authority vis-a-vis the population. Before the time of Martanda Varma rebellion was the recognised form of protest and Malabar law did not allow either confiscation of property or even capital punishment in the case of nobles. But after the firm organisation of Travancore, rebellion as a political weapon and warfare as a national habit disappeared from Malabar history.

That policy was followed with great success in Cochin by Paliath Komu Achan, the greatest name in the annals of that state. He reduced the nobles and took away their feudal privileges. This was all the more remarkable in his case, as Paliyam was the most important of the feudal nobility of the state. Komu Achan did not hesitate to sacrifice the interests of his order for the good of Cochin and his firm hand converted what was a nominal suzereinty over warring chieftains into an effective political authority over the present territories of Cochin.

This transformation marked the end of Nayar predominance in Malabar. From a privileged order which through its local chiefs controlled the affairs of Malabar, the Nayars in Travancore and Cochin became merely the chief community in these states. Their political power as a community was completely broken. In the territories of the Zamorins and Kolathiris their influence continued for a few more years. The invasion of Hyder Ali swept away much besides Nayar political power before it. And with the annexation of Malabar by the British by the treaty of Seringapatam the same policy which Martanda Varma had initiated in Travancore and Komu Achan followed in Cochin, was carried with relentless vigour. The second half of the 18th century thus witnessed the destruction of the political predominance of the Nayars and this is the most capital fact in the history of Malabar during the last 400 years.

Economically Malabar underwent great change, during the Dutch period. The raising of the Portuguese blockade, and the consequent freedom of commerce permitted by the Dutch led to a revival of Malabar trade. Ships from the Red Sea, Mocha Gujerat, and even China came to Malabar ports. The competition of the other European nations was also an incentive to commerce. The major rulers, especially the Zamorin and the Rajah of Travancore zealously encouraged trade and did everything in their power to increase it. This naturally led to a great activity at the various ports, especially Cochin, Colachel and Calicut.

The Dutch did much to improve cultivation and to introduce new products. Both cocoanut and rice the Company itself cultivated extensively. In the small scattered properties of the Company there were no less than 49,000 fruit bearing cocoanut trees. In fact, Baipeen was so closely planted that according to Moens its military value became greatly diminished. They introduced better methods of cocoanut cultivation and improved seeds. In Vendurty alone, they had 4990 trees. In Kalliakad, an island lying between Kayamkulam and Quilon they had 5462. Even now in the areas formerly cultivated by the Dutch the cocoanuts are better in quality. Following their example the entire coast took to cocoanut cultivation, especially because both coir and cocoanut oil were in great demand. Rice cultivation also derived much encouragement from the Dutch. But much of the rice that was consumed in Malabar was imported from Canara.

The Dutch introduced indigo cultivation into Malabar. Though this plant is native to the soil in Malabar its commercial cultivation had not been undertaken before. The Dutch thought that much profit could be made by an extensive cultivation of indigo and for the purpose seedlings were brought from Surat and they were sown in Mangat country and in Ernakulam and attempts were made to continue the cultivation in earnest. The seeds were distributed in Vendurty, Chetwai, Pappanetty, Cranganore and Varapoly, and the Mukhavas were entrusted with the cultivation.

The Company also tried to cultivate a good many other Malabar products. Both by their improved methods and by their scientific system, the Dutch attempts at cultivation had great effect on economic conditions in Malabar. Cultivation improved and the coastal people took to plantation of cocoanuts for the purpose of trade and this introduction of commercial economy was highly beneficial to the population.

They also introduced many industries. Salt farming became one of the main industries of Malabar. The Company itself owned 19,700 salt pans and following them the Indian rulers introduced this industry which was very profitable. Another industry which the Dutch introduced and which took root in Malabar was that of dyeing. The community of dyers first came to Malabar from Tuticorin and was brought by a Canarese merchant Babu Prabhu. About 50 years later in the time of Gollenesse another community of dyers was encouraged to settle in Malabar and they received plots of ground for houses and were given other conveniences.

The revival of industries and the opening of ports led to a large increase in trade. The ports all over the Malabar coast naturally showed signs of prosperity. Cochin especially was until the end of the 18th century a very important port. James Forbes states that in 1770 Cochin was a place of great trade and presented a striking contrast to Goa; a harbour filled with ships, streets crowded with merchants, and warehouses stored with goods from every part of Asia and Europe, marked the industry, the commerce and wealth of the inhabitants. The following is the description of the city of Cochin under the Dutch given by Francis Day.

"The Dutch Cochin fort according to Stravonines

Oriental Memoirs 1834, I 207.

was nearly semi-circular and about a mile and a half in circumference. On the land-side were six large bastions and a cavelier to the eastward: an irregular work on a large scale on the water-side a substantial loop-holed wall terminating at its eastern extremity in a ravelin before the cavelier: a wet ditch ran round these works whilst before it was a covered way and glacis."[1]

The north or river-side was defended by batteries whilst a stone wharf or more properly speaking a plain wall was erected on the river face.

"The sea a west face protected by a ravelin, the east by morasses and by a strong wall, and the west by walls and a wet ditch. There were three small gates one to the west, the Bay Gate, another to the east called the New Gate and one to the north the River Gate. Along each side of the wider streets and ramparts were portia trees, Thespesia populnea, left by the Portuguese and under their grateful shade, the inhabitants of an evening lounged or promenaded. A small but elegant public garden was kept inside the fort and a larger one near the Governor's house; in the vicinity of which the richer classes possessed bungalows. . . . . The pieces of artillery in the fort consisted of 95 of iron, six of brass and two mortars. . . The buildings in the fort were the commandant's house on the north-west bastion and the only one built on the Dutch models. The Governor's house was half a mile to the south divided from the fort by a long sandy plain."[2]

1) Day—Land of the Perumals—1868—p. 125-6. 2) Ibid. 126.

The trade of Cochin—without including the business transacted by the Dutch which probably formed at least 90 p. c. of it—amounted to 5 lakhs. The total trade must have been much over half a crore and this, in terms of the rupee of to-day, was indeed a very considerable figure.

The other important ports on the coast, besides Calicut, whose trade was in a flourishing state up to Mysorean invasion, were Colachel and Quilon. The Travancore government founded a new port at Alleppey for foreign trade and it soon developed into an important centre of commerce. Quilon, Anjengo, Colachel, and Tengapatanam which were the main ports in the south, all of which except the first developed into important trading centres only after the decline of Portuguese power, exported mostly coir, cotton cloth, tamarind and jaggery. Kottar, which was a very ancient centre of piece-goods trade, maintained its predominance as it does to-day. Nieuhoff mentions it as a place of great traffic and Van Imhoff[1] also found it to be a place of importance.

In the 18th century, most of the inland towns and the local capitals of chiefs like Purakkad declined greatly as a result of the Travancorean conquest. We do not hear any more of the famous market of Kayamkulam, or about the trade of "Proca". The centralised administration of Travancore which established a state monopoly in all possible goods, diverted the trade from these ancient ports. As a consequence, the economic centre of gravity shifted from the centre of Malabar

1) Journal in Ms. No. 281 Madras Records.

to the south. It was to the south of Quilon that new towns arose and new ports except Alleppey became of importance. The most rapid rise was that of Trivandrum. At the beginning of the 17th century, it was but an insignificant town unknown to history except for its famous pagoda. At the end of the 17th century, it became the capital of the Travancore Rajahs, then practically prisoners of the Ettuveetil Nobles. But with the rise of Martanda Varma, Trivandrum became practically the capital of Malabar. Martanda Varma was a great builder. He planned the city and had it rebuilt to suit its altered position. The ancient pagoda was pulled down and the noble structure which now commands the city of Trivandrum was constructed, as a lasting witness to the King's architectural tastes. Wide roads were laid down and port facilities were developed, though the coast is shallow and not suitable as the site for a harbour. In fact, by the time of Martanda Varma's death, Trivandrum had usurped the place which Calicut had held all through Malabar history as the chief centre of Kerala. In the time of Martanda Varma's successor, Sri Rama Rajah Bahadur, Trivandrum was further beautified and made a much greater trading centre. His famous Prime Minister, Rajah Kesava Das, pursued a particularly enlightened policy with regard to trade and built just outside the fortress walls a commodious bazaar where foreign merchants were encouraged to come and settle down. For the trade of the northern districts, Kesava Das built a new port at Alleppey where better natural harbour facilities existed. Alleppey was laid out as a modern city, with wide streets and large bazaars. As it was situated on the southern end of the Vembanad backwater, it had excellent and cheap transport facilities for collecting up country produce for export. Alleppey continues to be a flourishing port even to-day and is next to Cochin the chief centre of Malabar trade.

Economic and political changes of this nature gave rise to far reaching changes in national character. In the course of the last fifty years of the 18th century, the population of Cochin and Travancore became peaceful cultivators of land instead of maintaining their livelihood by warfare. Swords and shields were thrown away and the Nayars took to ploughing the soil and improving their land. In national habits also there were remarkable changes. Tobacco became a universal habit in Malabar. The Jaffna leaf had become almost a necessity with every person in Travancore, even more than food and drink. Their habit was to chew tobacco with betel leaf, a habit which still persists all over Malabar. Its prevalence among all classes of people made the demand for it imperative. Of the whole produce of Jaffna tobacco, Travancore used to take 3/5ths of the entire quantity. For a long time the Travancore price was the standard price of the article on the market. The use of opium also was prevalent at the beginning of the Dutch period. Nieuhoff states[1] "They use amfion very greedily. They take the quantity of the bigness of a pea. This they either mix with arrack or chew alone sometimes,

1) Churchill 233.

till they fall asleep .... Some of them are accustomed to use amfion every day: some every two or three days." But the use of opium declined greatly during the century. The Dutch had stipulated by contract for a monopoly of the supply of opium, but they gave up the trade in it as they found the demand in Java much greater and consequently the profits also much higher. After about 1730 opium was scarce in Malabar and its use became exceptional.

Intoxicants were freely used. The favourite drink of the people was cocoanut toddy. The satirical poets of the age always accused the non-Brahmin castes of being addicted to drink. It is also known that many distinguished Brahmin scholars did not disdain this drink, though it was prohibited by their religion. The observant Nieuhoff noted that the Malabaris "distil a spirit called Arack out of the liquor but it is not near so good nor wholesome as our brandy" which no doubt is a matter of opinion. Foreign liquors also acquired some popularity, mostly among Syrian Christians but the use of brandy and wines owing to the prohibitive cost did not affect the masses.

Another important change in national habits was in clothing. When the Portuguese first visited Malabar, in fact, till the first quarter of the 18th century, even the upper classes of society wore only a loin cloth of muslin. The ordinary people used coarser country stuff. As a result of Mohommedan influences from Trichinopoly, the higher classes began to wear clothes in the north Indian fashion, long achkans and pyjamas and turbans on the head. This was the official costume of the Travancore and Cochin courts till recently.

It is natural that the eventful 18th century should have witnessed considerable change in the condition of the various sections that constituted Malabar society. The spiritual predominance of the *Nambudiries* continued unquestioned. Their position as Jenmies and as the sacred caste suffered no alteration. In Travancore, Martanda Varma was able to assert his royal authority over them in matters affecting the state, but only at the cost of abject spiritual surrender. The punishment that was meted out to him for taking away the temporal authority of Brahmin rulers like those of Purakkad and Tiruvella was a penance of 56 days and religious ceremonies to be conducted by *Nambudiries* at great expense to the state. These ceremonies continue with undiminished pomp even now.

The position of the Nayars, as noticed before, underwent an almost revolutionary change. No longer was Malabar the free field of Nayar ambition. Their territorial authority was extinguished by the conquests of Martanda Varma, the policy of Komu Achan and the invasion of Hyder Ali. But they continued to be the most influential community as a result of their extensive landed possessions and local prestige. Their *kalaris* fell into disuse and the organisation of the *kara* existed only for social purposes. The Nayar aristocracy, deprived of military and political power, lived entirely on its old traditions and the Kaimals, Kartavus and Panikkars maintained their dignity and their style for a considerable time longer merely by the force of tradition.

But the days of their unrestrained power were gone never to return.

Of the condition of the Syrian Christians during this period, there is ample material for a detailed history. For our purpose it is sufficient to summarise here the religious schisms that affected the growth of this important community. The Latin Christians on the coast, as we have already said, were subject to the Company, but the Syrian Christians were not. Governor Moens says emphatically "The Company never had any authority, nor could have, over the St. Thomas Christians, who were always subject to the country princes. Not even the Portuguese exercised any jurisdiction over them, although they did their utmost with the consent of the king of Cochin, to make these Christians accept the doctrines of Rome and acknowledge the hierarchy of the Pope."

The Syrian Christians at the time of the Dutch conquest were much divided among themselves. The Synod of Diamper had theoretically united the Syrian Church with Rome and brought the Christians of Malabar under the authority of the Pope. Even before the Portuguese flag ceased to fly over Malabar, revolt had broken out in the community. In 1640 they approached the Jacobite Patriarch of Antioch, the Patriarch of the Copts and the Nestorian Patriarch of Babylon to send a prelate. In 1644 a Syrian Bishop by the name of Ahballa was sent out to Malabar by the Patriarch of Antioch but the Portuguese came to know of it and interpreted him on the way and it was widely rumoured that he was thrown into the sea with a stone round his neck. On hearing this a considerable section of the community met at Mattanchery and decided to break away from Rome. They elected their own Bishop Mar Thoma Campo who maintained a precarious position until the Patriarch of Antioch sent in 1655 two Bishops, Mar Basilus and Mar Johannes, who established the authority of the Patriarch in Malabar. But a hopeless schism divided the Church. A great majority remained faithful to Rome, and the Bishops who were sent out from Antioch did not find it very easy to carry on their duties or even to organise their flock. Besides this fundamental difficulty, even the non-Roman Christians were not united in points of doctrine. There were two parties, one Nestorian and another Eutychian or Jacobite, who were fighting theological battles among themselves. The Jacobite Bishop Mar Thoma invited the Patriarch of Antioch to send three Bishops in order to strengthen the anti-Nestorian party but their arrival was the cause of further strife among the Jacobites. As soon as the Bishops arrived Mar Thoma turned against them and denounced them as heretics and though the commandeur supported the Syrian Bishops nothing could be done to force Mar Thoma to accept them. The Bishops and the commandeur turned to Martanda Varma in the same way as Alexis de Meneses had turned to the Rajah of Cochin and invoked his help. Martanda Varma recognised the Syrian Bishops and Mar Thoma was forced for the

Richard Collins : Missionary Enterprise in the East.
H. S. King Co. 1873, p. 77.

time to yield an unwilling obedience. But as soon as Martanda Varma died, Thoma represented the matter to the new Maharajah and again refused to recognise the Syrian Bishops whom he denounced publicly as heretics. This controversy continued for over 30 years and weakened the Church. It was only in 1773 after the death of Mar Thoma, who was succeeded by his nephew, that Governor Moens was able to reconcile both factions and restore peace.

The Syrian Christians like the Nayars were mostly cultivators of the soil and their economic condition was then as now fairly prosperous. Moens noted that "the houses of these Christians are not mixed up with those of the other Malabaris, but they have separate quarters where they live among themselves ...... They do not mix or intermarry with newly converted Christians of lower castes or classes. The majority of them belong to the Nayar caste or class of nobles and for this reason they, like Nayars, carry a sword in the hand as a token of their dignity."[1] Their priesthood at that time was not particularly educated, except in the case of the Catholics for whose benefit the Jesuits had established excellent colleges at Verapoly. But the influence of the Kattanars with their flock was very great as Alexis de Meneses and later on the Bishops from Syria discovered to their cost.

The Mohammedan community lost its importance in the politics and trade of Malabar with the fall of the Kunjalis. There were important families here and there, but in the general affairs of the country they ceased to

1) Moens, p. 178.

count till the invasion of Hyder Ali. A hundred years of warfare with the Portuguese had reduced them to insignificance in Malabar and when the Dutch were installed in Cochin and gained control of the Malabar trade they did not meet with any effective competition from the Mohammedan merchants. The days of Mammalis and Kuttialis were over. The Moorish population on the coast and the families inland became merely another section of Malabar population. From this insignificant position they again rose to some importance in the territories lying to the north of Cochin at the time of Hyder Ali's invasion.

The position of the untouchable castes remained much the same during this period. It would not, however, be correct to assume that though the Thiyas suffered from social disabilities their position was altogether unimportant. They were an important factor in the life of Malabar and were utilised for military purposes by the Company. There were many scholars of considerable standing among them, and one of them, Itty Atchutan, was among the valued collaborators of Henrick Van Rheede in compiling the monumental work, *Hortus Malabaricus*.

The eighteenth century witnessed a remarkable revival in Malayalam literature. The Rajahs of the time were great patrons of literature, especially the last Rajah of Purakkad and the Travancore Maharajahs, Martanda Varma and his successor Rama Varma. In the court of the Rajah of Purakkad lived the great Kunchan Nambiar who is justly esteemed one of the greatest of Malayalam poets. When Martanda Varma conquered Purakkad, he carried off with him the poet as his richest booty and installed him at Trivandrum. In the reign of his successor, who was one of the most accomplished scholars of his time in India, the Trivandrum court became justly famous all over Hindustan as the centre of scholarship, culture and wit. A nod from the Rajah of Travancore, says a Sanskrit Sloka, is more valuable than a lakh of rupees from any other Rajah. Moens, who had occasion to talk with the Maharajah, states that he conversed fluently in English, read the papers and periodicals published in London, Calcutta and Madras and was generally well informed in European affairs. He was a poet of great distinction and in his court resided Kunchan Nambiar, Unnayi Warriyar and other great writers of Malabar.

Education was fairly widespread during the 18th century. Malabar always had an efficient system of village schools at which elementary education was imparted free to all comers. Malabar was the home of Sanskrit scholarship in the 18th century and the *kavyas*, dramas and grammatical works in Sanskrit produced at that time in Malabar will bear comparison to the work produced at any time after the golden age of Sanskrit. Medicine especially was studied extensively. For Christians there were special institutions maintained by Carmelite friars near Cranganore. For a certain number education was given free in Latin and Syriac. The students were taught, besides these languages, theology, mathematics and geography.

While the economic results of the contact with the Dutch were undeniably beneficial to Malabar on its cultural side, it was altogether barren. It is noteworthy that the educational and other institutions which continued to have influence over a section of Malabar population, were maintained almost entirely by the Catholic Orders. It was neither Portugal nor Holland but Rome that attempted to bring education to Malabar. The Dutch founded neither libraries, nor colleges, nor were they interested in anything except their trade. But they were diligent observers and their memoirs, accounts and letters form one of the main sources of our knowledge of Malabar. Besides this, an indirect contribution of higher importance to the culture of Malabar was the compilation of *Hortus Malabaricus* under the direction of Henrick Van Rheede which together with Orta's *Colloquies* may be said to constitute the first attempt at scientific research concerning India. The accounts left by Linschoten, Nieuhoff, Stavorinus, Baldeus and others also from an indirect contribution to Malabar on which is based most of our present day information of the condition of Malabar in the latter half of the 17th century.

The 18th century marked definite advancement in various directions in Malabar. Trade and commerce improved greatly and became stable. The economic condition of the masses also improved leading to much higher standard of living. Political organisation also underwent great changes. A new state with different ideals and ambitions came into existence and the old feudal anarchy disappeared over a large part of Malabar. In all this, except in the stabilisation of trade, the Dutch had hardly any part. It was in spite of their active opposition that Travancore annexed the smaller lords between Cochin and Quilon. Nothing would have suited the Dutch better than that feudal anarchy should reign in Malabar. Thus if 18th century saw Malabar making rapid advance it was in no way due to the presence of the Dutch. Their position was limited and their activities circumscribed. Within the limits they imposed on themselves, their activities were directed, it must be admitted, to the betterment of Malabar.

CHAPTER XII

CONCLUSION

With the conquest of Cochin by the British even the last relic of the connection of Hollanders with Malabar vanished. Their political power had ended a full half-century before.

The Dutch period witnessed remarkable political, social and economic changes in Malabar, some of which have been discussed in the preceding chapters. Except in the economic changes where their influence was immediate, they played no direct part. In the political sphere the part that the Dutch played was important only in the sense that their defeat and eclipse were necessary before the boundaries of Travancore could be changed and the minor feudatories brought under control.

At the same time it cannot be said that their contact with Malabar was barren of results. They actively promoted industry, introduced artisans into the country and, at least in one very important case, took great interest in Indian learning. Van Rheede's *Hortus Malabaricus* would by itself make the Dutch connection with Malabar memorable, while the activities of Gollenesse, Moens and others to improve the cotton fabrics of Malabar and to introduce better systems of dyeing and printing entitle them to the gratitude of Malayalees.

Unlike the Portuguese, the Dutch never claimed

that they had conquered India or any portion of it. As their pretensions were less and their desire to do profitable trade evident, they caused less friction and created less trouble than the Portuguese. The Portuguese from the time of da Gama appointed governors and viceroys to govern the East. The Dutch were satisfied with commandeurs and factors. Their connection with Malabar was not marred by any of those atrocious deeds of barbarism which made Portuguese name a bye-word in the East. Calculating, matter of fact, and well trained in the doubtful art of diplomacy, the Dutch presented a striking contrast to the arrogant and incompetent Portuguese whose finances were always on the brink of bankruptcy but whose pretensions were never less than those of universal dominion and empire.

The end of the Dutch was inglorious. That was hardly surprising. A full half century before the end came they had lost all the vestiges of political power. The rise of Travancore and the invasion of Hyder Ali had made them impotent on land. The absolute mastery of the Indian seas which the English gained, after the great Suffren withdrew from the Indian waters, and the authority which the English East India Company came to possess on the mainland with the end of the 18th century, rendered the position of the Dutch totally dependent on the favour of the British. After the Treaty of Mavelikkara their attitude towards Malabar princes was one of nervous neutrality. With the invasion of Hyder Ali it changed into one of servile subservience towards the Mysore power. When the power of Tipu was destroyed in Malabar and the Company annexed the broad domains of the Zamorin, the Dutch settlement in Cochin was merely an unimportant trading centre. Its conquest by the British came in the natural course of events and was not marked by any heroic defence as the Portuguese even in their decadence had put up against Goens. The continuance or disappearance of Cochin as a Dutch settlement had come to mean little for Malabar. If the British had spared it, the port would have continued like Mahe or Chandernagore, a foreign possession of no importance—a historical and picturesque survival of an interesting period of history.

APPENDIX 1.

The translation of a treaty of Alliance entered into by the Rajah of Cochin under his signature with the Rajah of Travancore.

Directions written by Pandel Hicomen, Mootseddy of Cochin and addressed to Puducherry Mootseddy of Travancore, dated 12th day of Dhanu of Malabar year 937, 22nd December, 1761, viz.:

In the treaty of agreement made at Trivandrum on the 12th day of Makarom of the year 932 (the 22nd January 1757) the capitulations already drawn at Mavelikkara, the 3rd of Chingom 936 (15th August 1760) for the future formation of an alliance are included. The terms mentioned therein were, that the former discords being settled it is agreed to continue for ever friends, that we shall support and assist each other both in good and bad fortune, that the mutual friendship of the parties may be preserved in the same manner already agreed on, that none of the people, who deserted from Travancore country, shall be allowed to remain in my dominions, nor be supported in any manner, that the agent of Travancore Rajah shall be allowed to purchase on the Rajah's account from the country merchants for ready money all the pepper produced within the limits of my dominions, except 500 candies annually wanted for my own trade for collecting which it is stipulated that a certain place shall be ascertained; it will be taken from thence by my merchant accounting first to your merchant kept for the same purpose.

Since the time of conclusion of this agreement it was agreed that the money expended on account of the troubles raised by the Chempakasherry and Vadakkumkur Chiefs shall be recovered from them, that until the said payment is duly made the Rajah of Travancore is empowered to collect the revenues of both their districts, that I will never in future afford them any assistance, that Chempakasherry remain at Trishchmeereo according to Rajah's permission, that while he remains there I will by no means write to nor accept any letter from him nor supply him with money for his expenses nor have any interview with him, that besides this I will not keep in my country anyone that hath ill behaved towards the Rajah and that all the superintendence of both parties in the Pagodas of both countries may be kept in practice the same as before.

All the aforesaid Articles of Agreement having been made in writing, the Zamoorin entered with his army into my country and expelling my people took possession of my country on which account in attention to my request the Rajah ought to assist me with money and his army in expelling my enemy from my property until the possession of it shall be restored to me, the north boundary of which on the west side being limited to the southward of Poocoida and on the east side to the southward of Chiltur as also the villages of Bella Ponatara formerly belonging to me. In recompense, therefore, of the above required assistance I give it up in writing the districts of Karappuram (except the villages named Audicadu, Chettany and Cumballon) situated to the southward of Pompolly and to the northward of Alipee as also all the districts annexed to it Paroor and Alangadoo I do wish the Rajah may profit by them accordingly, with all the rights and profits belonging to them.

Until the Rajah's troops are called from my dominions, where they remain now for its defence, the half amount of the revenue that my people should collect from my countries I shall duly pay for the expenses of the said troops.

In case of the Rajah's troops entering into Vellapadcara country he may take the revenue of that country appointing his own men in like manner that the Zamoorin formerly collected it.

If required the Rajah will support me with every assistance of troops and money until the enemies are repulsed and the countries restored to me.

Excepting the districts situated to the northward of Murinhapaya and to the southward of Varapole containing the districts within the Charinadu already possessed by the Rajah until the year 933 (1757) all the rest I will myself take charge of.

The Rajah will assist me agreeably to my design in abolishing the dignities of every rank in my country as also in the concerns appertaining to them.

All the contents herein written you may read and impart to the Rajah of Travancore entitled Culasheghara Perumal.

(*Sd.*) RAJAH OF COCHIN.

APPENDIX 2.

The translation of an agreement entered into by the Rajah of Travancore with the Rajah of Cochin under the 12th Dhanu 937 Malabar Style.

On the 12th Makarom 932 an agreement took place between us the particulars of which had been settled by the parties at Mavelikkara. On the 3rd Chingom 929 it was there agreed that the parties should lay aside all former enmity which subsisted between them and observe and cultivate a perpetual friendship with each other. In conformity to that agreement I engage that I will not protect or afford any assistance whatever to your enemies in my country. As you wish to receive 500 candies of pepper out of the produce of your country at any place you may think proper, I have only to request that your merchant or broker may receive the quantity with the consent and in the presence of my merchant, and my merchant shall advance money and receive the remainder of the pepper produced in your country as soon as this agreement shall have taken place. The Chief of Chempakasherry, Ambalapilly, Vadakkumkur have been indisposed towards me and you promise not to take part with them. The sums expended by me in reducing them to subjection shall be levied from them and that until the amount be paid I shall retain the possession of their districts in my own hands and you promise not to take part with them or render them any assistance. As I place much confidence in this assurance on your part, I have agreed that the Chief of Ambalapilly etc., shall be permitted to remain at Trichoor and during the period of their residence at that place you promise not to hold any correspondence with them by letter or otherwise, nor to afford them any supplies for their subsistence nor to have any interview with them; you further promise not to grant protection to my enemies in your country. In regard to certain privileges which you possess in my country and some also which I possess in your country they must be observed and continued as has ever been the custom.

All the aforesaid articles having been agreed to, you inform me that the Samoory has entered your country with his troops, expelled your people and taken possession of it and you desire me to assist you by sending my troops at my own expense in order to enable you to recover possession of your country by expelling the Samoory's troops from that part which extends north as far as Poocoida river and east as far as Chitoor river as also the districts you formerly possessed in Vellapanad Karee. If I should assist you and put you in possession of this country in return you agree to make over to me the districts Karappuram extending to the south of Pampolly river and north of Alipie and also Paroor and Alangadoo with all their rights, etc., except the three villages Chetany, Yeado and Chambalam and you further agree to pay into the hands of my people the amount of half of the revenues in the villages formerly belonging to the Samoory in the same manner as Samoory collected them. I will send my troops to be paid by me and will use every exertion and render all the assistance in my power to defeat Samoory's troops and restore your country. You shall be put in possession of those villages which were not conquered by me in the year 988 in the districts of Charinadoo extending north as far as Turinhapaya river and south as far as Verapole river. When you wish to discharge the petty Polygars in your country, I will join you and render you all the assistance in my power, I desire that Dewauree may read and explain this agreement to the Elder Rajah Parumpadapoo. The agreement is drawn up by Sankara Coomaran by order of the Travancore Rajah.

(Signed) TRAVANCORE RAJAH.

APPENDIX 3.

Propositions of the Dutch Commandeur.	Answer of the English Commander.
The Governor-in-Council of Cochin proposes to Major Petrie, of the 77th Regiment, and commanding the Detachments of the King's, and East India Company's troops, to surrender this place, on the 20th of this month, and requests at the same time, that all hostilities may cease.	The garrison of Cochin will be prisoners, and the Fort given over to his Great Britannic Majesty tomorrow noon, at 12 O'clock, at which time, the Bay-gate, and the New Gate shall be delivered over to such detachments, as Major Petrie will order to take possession of them.
Article 1st The Officers of the Garrison, and the Military, that have defended Cochin will, with all the honours of war, march out from the Bay-gate, together with their arms, baggage, flying colours, beating of drums, and lighted matches, as also two cannon, with their appurtenances.	The Garrison will march out as requested, and lay down their arms on the Esplanade, when they must return back, as prisoners of war.

Article 2nd

All officers and soldiers, which are of the Garrison of Cochin, will with as little delay as possible, be transported either to Batavia, or Ceylon, at the expense of the English Government in English vessels.	Cannot be granted; about the Garrison, it will be disposed of as the Commander-in-Chief may deem proper.

Article 3rd

The said officers, and soldiers will take with them all their effects, without their being liable to any search. Their servants, and slaves; whilst those that are married, will likewise be at liberty to take their families with them.	Allowed, excepting with respect to slaves, a name unknown in the British dominions.

Article 4th

The Governor, the Members of Council, and all the servants of Police, and Trade, Churchmen, Military and Naval, and other servants, in the pay of the Dutch Company as also all the inhabitants of Cochin, either Europeans, or natives will be at liberty to hold their persons, and property, movable and immovable, merchandise and other effects without being therein molested, or obstructed, on any account whatsoever.	All private property will be sacred.

Article 5th

Among the foregoing, is also understood, regarding the liberty of the Factor, and Resident of Porca, J. A. Scheits, who is now employed here, in keeping the Company's mercantile books and he must be allowed to return to his station, to resume his office.

A reasonable time will be allowed him, to settle his affairs but he must be considered as a prisoner of war.

Article 6th

The Governor, the Members of Council and all the servants of Police, and trade, the Churchmen and further servants in pay, will be at liberty to take their families, male and female slaves and also their possessions, either to Batavia or Columbo, and they will be granted thereto, at the expense of the British Government, the necessary ships and transport.

This is replied to in the 2nd article.

Article 7th

The funds belonging to the Orphan College, and the Poor House will not be confiscated or seized upon, they being money of orphans and the poor.

The funds mentioned in this article will belong to his Great Britannic Majesty, in so far that he will appoint persons over them, for their management.

Article 8th

All officers, and servants, Civil and Political, of the Company, who may wish to remain at this place, as private individuals, shall be granted the protection of the British flag.

All the inhabitants, who are willing to remain and to take the oath of allegiance to his Great Britannic Majesty, will in every respect, be treated as British subjects.

Article 9th

All mercantile articles, ammunitions, artillery, goods, arms, provisions and other articles, which belong to the Company, and are found at this place, will faithfully be made over, according to a specific statement, to the commissaries that will be appointed to receive them, and the specified list, will in duplicate, be duly delivered to Major Petrie.

Everything mentioned in this article, will be faithfully delivered over to such persons as Major Petrie will appoint hereafter, to dispose, thereabout agreeably to the direction of his Great Britannic Majesty.

Article 10th

The fortifications, the Government House, all magazines, and other public buildings, belonging to the Company, will be kept as

Regarding the Fort of Cochin and other public buildings, they

they are at present, and not be demolished.	will be disposed of as the Commander-in-Chief or the Commanding Officer, will think proper at the time.
Article 11th	
The free exercise of the reformed religion, as usual in the Dutch Church, where Divine Service is performed, will be permitted.	Allowed.
Article 12th	
The Convent at Verapoly, and all other Romish Churches, as also the Heathen Temples, will receive the protection, that they have hitherto enjoyed, under the Dutch Company.	The British Government everywhere protects religious exercises.
Article 13th	
All Topazes (half castes) and Inland Christians, as also the Banians, Silversmiths, who are subjects and vassals of the Dutch Company, will retain their property and also privileges and protections which they always had enjoyed, of the said Company.	Answered in the 4th and 8th Articles.
Article 14th	
All documents, charters, Resolutions, and other papers, belonging	All Public Documents and pa-

to this Government, will without any search being made of them, be delivered over to the Governor, Mr. Van Spall, in order to be carried with him, wherever he may be removed to.	pers must be delivered to persons appointed to receive them but Mr. Van Spall will have authenticated vouchers of those which may in any way concern himself during his management of Cochin.
Article 15th	
No one will occupy the Govt. House during (his) Mr. Spall's stay at Cochin but he will remain unmolested.	Answered in 4th Article.
Article 16th	
In case of any English Deserters being found in the Garrison of Cochin, they will be pardoned.	All deserters will absolutely be given over.
Article 17th	
All public papers, notarial or Secretariat deeds, which may in the least, be to the security of the possessions, belonging to the inhabitants of this place, will be respected and preserved, in the hands of those, who hold that office, in order to be made use of, whenever required.	Answered in the 14th Article.

Article 18th

The Auctioner of the Town, the Sequester and the Curator (Trustees) will be supported in the recovering of all outstanding money, and be therein protected, by the usual officers of Justice.

All inhabitants who remain in Cochin, will be subject to British laws.

Article 19th

After this capitulation shall have been signed, the New-gate shall be made over to an English Detachment, of 50 men, to which an equal number of Dutch soldiers may go out and no English one may rush in, and the next day all the gates will be taken possession of by the English troops and the Garrison of Cochin will retire to a certain place, and remain there until their departure for Batavia, or Ceylon, laying down their arms, as usual, with the exception of the officers commanding them who will retain their swords.

The Gates of the Fort of Cochin will be taken possession of, by a detachment of British troops, tomorrow noon, at 12 O'clock. The Garrison will be lodged as conveniently as the circumstances will allow until it can be disposed of thereabout, agreeably to the second Article. The officers may retain their swords.

Article 20th

All servants of the Company, the Police, Military, Navy and others in pay, will be supported by the

Major Petrie is of opinion that he has not the autho-

English Govt. until they are taken in English vessels, to the place of their destination, either Batavia or Colombo.	rity to enter into such an agreement. Part of this Article has been answered in Art. 2.

Article 21st

All sick and wounded, now in the Hospital, are to be treated, and maintained, by the English Government.	Allowed.
The fulfilment of all the above stated articles, and the manner of capitulation agreed to, are to be faithfully observed and signed respectively, by Major Petrie, the Governor Van Spall, and the Council of this place.	Major Petrie consents to a cessation of Arms at which time, Mr. Van Spall should declare whether or not he will accept the aforementioned articles of capitulation.
19th October, 1795.	11. 30 p. m. 19th October, 1795.
(Sd.) J. L. VAN SPALL, P. J. DECAN, I. A. CELLARIUS, I. H. SCHEIDS, A. LUNEL, C. VAN SPALL.	*(Sd.)* G. PETRIE *Major 77th Regiment Commanding.*

APPENDIX 4.

Jan. 8th 1663	—	Dutch conquer Cochin
March 20, ,,	—	Treaty with the Rajah of Cochin
1689	--	Adoption into the Cochin family
1691	—	Chetwai ceded to the Zamorin
1697	—	Cochin fort reduced
1701	—	War declared between the Zamorin and Cochin
1714	—	Chetwai Fort destroyed by the Zamorin
1715	—	Zamorin invaded Cochin and occupied Trichur
1717	—	Peace with the Zamorin
1739	—	Death of the Rajah of Quilon
1753	—	Peace between the Dutch and Travancore
1762	—	Travancore defeats the Zamorin
1766	—	Hyder Ali conquers Malabar
Nov. 13, 1776	—	Dutch fort at Chetwai surrenders to Sirdar Khan
1778	—	Dutch attack Cranganore (under Mysore)
March 3, 1778	—	Dutch defeated
1789	—	Fort of Cranganore sold by the Dutch to Travancore
Oct. 19, 1795	—	Fortress of Cochin surrendered to the British
1814	—	Town of Cochin finally surrendered

APPENDIX 5.

The list of regular Commandeurs in Cochin begins only with Van Rheede. Immediately after the capture the fort was placed under Commissioners.

Hendrick Adriaan Van Rheede	1673-77	[Baron Hendrick Adriaan Van Rheede (d. at Surat Dec. 15, 1691) author of the *Hortus Malabaricus.*]
Jacob Lobo	1677-78	
Martin Huysman	1680-81	
Gulmer Vorsbuy	1684-1686	
Isaak Van Dielen	1687-1693	Van Dielen (d. at Cochin Dec. 25, 1693). Adriaan Van Ommen (d. Nov. 27, 1696 at Cochin).
Hendrik Zwaadekroon	1693-1698	
Peter Cocsaart—acting	1698	
Magnes Wickelman	1698-1701	
W. Moerman	1705-1709	
Barent Ketel	1709-1716	
Johannes Hertinberg	1717-1724	
Jakob De Jong	1724-1731	

Adriaan Van Maten	1731-1735
J. Stein Van Gollenesse	1735-1743
Siersma	1743-1748
C. Stevens	1748-1750
Abraham Cornelis de la Haye	1750-1751
C. Cunes	1751-1757
C. De Jong	1757-1761
Godfried Wayerman	1761-1764
C. Breekpot	1764-1769
C. L. Snett	1769-1771
Adrian Moens	1771-1781
G. Anglebeck	1781-1793
Jan Lambertus Van Spall	1793-1795

APPENDIX 6.

The main Dutch Tombs on the West Coast are described by Mr. J. J. Cotton in his book on Indian Monumental Inscriptions Vol. III, Madras (p. 267). The reader who is interested is referred to that excellent work. A list of the more important personages is given below. The Tombstones are mainly in the Church of St. Francis, and in the Dutch Cemetery.

Isaak Van Dialen—died on the 25th December, 1693.

Commander-in-Chief of the Dutch forces on the Coast.

Adrian Van Ommen—died 27th November, 1696.

Commander-in-Chief of the Coast.

Hester Dulcina de Jong—died 4th December, 1727.

Wife of Jacob de Jong, Governor of Cochin.

Gustaf and Urusula Van Gollenesse—Gustaf died on the 30th March and Urusula 3rd of May, 1739, children of Governor Gollenesse.

Abraham Cornelis De La Haye—died 5th October, 1752.

De La Haye was Governor of Cochin (1850-1).

The tombstones of the above are in St. Francis' Church.

John Adam Cellarius—died 15th June, 1796. Was one of the signatories of the Capitulation of Cochin. Buried in the Dutch Cemetery at Cochin.

Wilhelm Blasser—died 2nd February, 1729. Died at the Chetwai fort of which he was Captain. A slab was discovered in the fort leaving an inscription.

AIYER.—*Indian Constitutional Problems.* By Sir P. S. Sivaswamy Aiyer, K. C. S. I., C. I. E. Rs. 7-8.

ARNOLD.—*Through India with a Camera.* An album of 100 photographic views of its famous cities and natural scenery. With descriptive notes by Sir T. W. Arnold, in two bindings. Cloth Rs. 5. Paper Rs. 4.

AYYAR.—*Indian After-Dinner Stories.* A collection of 240 witty and humorous stories of Indian life, customs and manners. By A. S. P. Ayyar, M. A. (Oxon.), I. C. S. 2 Vols. Each Rs. 4.

. . . .—*Sense in Sex, and other Droll Stories of Intrigues and Amours of Indian Women.* By A. S. P. Ayyar, M. A. (Oxon.), I. C. S. Rs. 4.

. . . . . .—*Baladitya.* A Historical Romance of Ancient India. By A. S. P. Ayyar, M. A. (Oxon.), I. C. S. Fully Illustrated. Rs. 4.

. . . .—*Great Short Stories of India.* By A. S. P. Ayyar, M. A. (Oxon.), I. C. S. Rs. 5.

. . . .—*An Indian in Western Europe.* By A. S. P. Ayyar, M. A. (Oxon.), I. C. S. Two Volumes, bound in one. Rs. 4.

BACHCHA.—*Easy Hindustani for Europeans.* By Chhota Bachcha. Revised by S. Ismail F. Idrus. Re. 1-14.

BEST SHORT STORIES OF INDIA.—An Anthology of Folk-Tales of the various Provinces of India. Reprinted from "The Indian Antiquary". Two volumes.

BHANDARKAR.—*A Peep into the Early History of India.* By Sir R. G. Bhandarkar, M. A., Ph. D., K. C. I. E. With a Preface by H. G. Rawlinson, Principal, Karnatak College, Dharwar. Second Edition. Rs. 2.

BHARUCHA.—*Zoroastrian Religion and Customs*: A Brief Sketch. By E. S. D. Bharucha, Fellow of the University of Bombay. With an Introduction by Dr. J. J. Modi, B. A., Ph. D., C. I. E. Third Edition, Revised and Enlarged. Rs. 3.

BLATTER AND ALMEIDA.—*Ferns of Bombay.* A handbook on the Culture of many of the most widely distributed and rare species of Ferns in the Bombay Presidency. By E. Blatter, S. J., Ph. D., F. L. S. and J. F. D'Almeida, B. A., B. Sc. (Hon.), Professors of Botany, St. Xavier's College, Bombay. With numerous illustrations coloured and black-and-white. Rs. 7-8.

BOMBAY THROUGH A CAMERA. An album of Bombay pictures, 98 in number, beautifully reproduced on buff art paper. Re. 1.

CHORDIA.—*Chitor, and Other Poems.* By Shyam Sundar Lal Chordia. Foreword by E. E. Speight, Professor of English Literature, Osmania College, Hyderabad. Rs. 4.

CHUDGAR.—*Indian Princes Under British Protection.* A Study of their Personal Rule, their Constitutional Position, and their Future. By P. L. Chudgar, Bar.-at-Law. With a Preface by Col. Wedgewood. Rs. 4.

CHATTERJI.—*A Plea for Open-Air Schools in India.* By S. C. Chatterji, B. Sc., L. T., M. Ed., Lecturer, Government Training College, Ajmer. Re. 1-8.

CHIPLUNKAR.—*The Scientific Basis of Women's Education.* By The Late Prof. G. M. Chiplunkar, Fellow of the Indian Women's University of Poona. Rs. 3.

DADACHANJI.—*History of Indian Currency and Exchange.* By Professor B. E. Dadachanji, M. A., Morris College, Nagpur. Rs. 2-14.

DATTA.—*Peasant-Proprietorship in India.* By Professor Dwijadas Datta, M. A., A. R. A. C. Rs. 3.

. . . .—*Land-Lordism in India.* By Prof. Dvijadas Datta, M. A., A. R. A. C. Rs. 3.

DAVAR.—*Elements of Indian Mercantile Law.* By Sohrab R. Davar, Bar.-at-Law, Principal and Founder of Davar's College of Commerce. Fifth Edition. Rs. 10.

. . . .—*Elements of Indian Company Law.* By Sohrab R. Davar, Bar.-at-Law. New Edition. Rs. 8.

DUBEY.—*The Indian Public Debt.* A critical study of the Borrowing Policy of the Government of India in Recent Times. By D. L. Dubey, M. A., Ph. D. Foreword by The Hon. Sir George Schuster. Rs. 8.

EDWARDES.—*Byways of Bombay.* By S. M. Edwardes, C. V. O., I. C. S. With twenty Illustrations by Rao Bahadur M. V Dhurandhar, Headmaster, Sir J. J. School of Art, Bombay Rs. 7-8.

FAVOURITE CHARACTERS FROM PICTURESQUE INDIA. An album of 23 coloured reproductions of the natives of India. Re. 1-12.

GEDGE AND CHOKSI.—*Women in Modern India.* Fifteen Essays on the status and achievements of Indian Women. Written by well-known Indian Women of all classes. Collected and Edited by Evelyn C. Gedge and Mithan Choksi, M. A. Foreword by Sarojini Naidu. Rs. 4.

GILES.—*The Motorists' Guide for India.* By M. J. Giles. With map. Rs. 3-8.

GUBBAY.—*Indigenous Indian Banking.* By M. M. S. Gubbay, C. S. I., C. I. E. Re. 1-12.

GUTHRIE.—*The Hymns of Zoroaster.* Translated with Introduction and Notes by K. S. Launfal Guthrie. Rs. 10.

HABIB.—*Sultan Mahmud of Ghaznin.* By Mohammad Habib, B. A. (Oxon.), Professor of History and Politics, Muslim University, Aligarh. Rs. 2-8.

. . . . . . —*Hazrat Amir Khusrau of Delhi.* By Mohammad Habib, B. A. (Oxon.) Rs. 2-8.

HILDRETH.—*Week-End Trips Around Bombay.* By Rail, Road, and Ferry Steamer. Described and Profusely Illustrated. By H. R. Hildreth, B. A. Re. 1-8.

HOYLAND AND BANERJEE.—*De Laet's "Empire of the Great Mogol".* Translation by Prof. J. S. Hoyland, M. A., F. R. Hist. S., with Annotations and Notes by Professor S. N. Banerjee, M. A. Rs. 5-8.

HURLIMANN.—*Picturesque India.* A Photographic Survey of the Land of Antiquity. Photographs and Introduction by Dr. Martin Hurlimann. (Three hundred and Four Photogravure Plates of Wonderful Monuments of India's Past Greatness, Beautiful Temples, Splendid Mosques, Gorgeous Tombs, Charming Waterfalls, Marvellous Fortifications and Pictures of various Types of People.) Rs. 20.

IYENGAR.—*Studies in Indian Rural Economics.* By Prof. S. Kesava Iyengar, M. A., F. R. E. S. Illustrated. Rs. 8.

KARANDIKAR.—*Hindu Exogamy.* A Scientific exposition of Hindu Marriage Customs. By S. V. Karandikar, M. A. Rs. 6.

KARKARIA.—*The Charm of Bombay.* By R. P. Karkaria. With a Foreword by H. E. Lord Willingdon, Late Governor of Bombay. Library Edition, Rs. 5; Popular Edition, Rs. 2-8.

KINCAID.—*The Tale of the Tulsi Plant, and Other Studies.* By The Hon. Mr. C. A. Kincaid, C. V. O., I. C. S. New Edition. Rs. 2-6.

. . . .—*Shri Krishna of Dwarka, and Other Stories.* By The Hon. Mr. C. A. Kincaid, C. V. O., I. C. S. Re. 1-8.

. . . .—*Folk Tales of Sind and Gujarat.* By The Hon. Mr. C. A. Kincaid, C. V. O., I. C. S. Re. 1-14.

KIRTIKAR.—*Studies in Vedanta.* By Rao Bahadur Vasudeva J. Kirtikar. Edited by M. R. Jayakar, M. A., LL. B., Bar.-at-Law. Rs. 14.

KRISHNAMOORTHY.—*Indian Practical Banking.* A Short Treatise on the Day-to-Day Working of a Joint Stock Bank. Foreword by G. Findlay Shirras, M. A. (Hon.), F. S. S., I. E. S. Second Edition. Rs. 2.

MANSHARDT.—*Bombay Today and Tomorrow.* Edited by The Rev. Clifford Manshardt, A. M., D. B., Ph. D. With an Introduction by The Rt. Hon'ble Sir Frederick Sykes, P. C., G. C. I. E., G. B. E., K. C. B., C. M. G. Rs. 4.

MEHTA.—*Studies in Indian Painting.* A Survey of Various Types of Indian Painting Ranging from the commencement of the seventh century to Circa 1870 A. D. By Nanalal Chamanlal Mehta, I. C. S. With 17 Plates in colour and numerous plates in Half-tone. Rs. 56.

MEHTA.—*Lord Hastings and the Indian States.* A Study of the Relations of the British Government in India with the Indian States from 1813-1823. By Dr. Mohan Sinha Mehta, M. A., LL. B., Ph. D., Bar.-at-Law. With a Foreword by Sir P. S. Sivaswamy Aiyer, K. C. S. I., C. I. E. Rs. 10.

MERCHANT.—*Income-Tax in Relation to Accounts.* By F. R. Merchant, F. S. A. A., Asst. Commissioner of Income-Tax, Bombay. Third Revised Edition. Rs. 6-4.

PANIKKAR.—*Sri Harsha of Kanauj:* The History of a Great Ruler of India in the first half of the 7th century A. C. By K. M. Panikkar, B. A. (Oxon.), Bar.-at-Law. Rs. 3-8.

PANIKKAR.—*The Working of Dyarchy in India.* By K. M. Panikkar, B. A. (Oxon.), Bar.-at-law, (nom-de-plume "Kerala Putra"). Rs. 4.

. . . .—*Malabar and the Portuguese.* A History of the Rise, Growth, Decline and Fall of the Portuguese in India from 1500 to 1663. By K. M. Panikkar, B. A. (Oxon.), Bar.-at-Law. Foreword by Lieut.-Col. Sir Richard Carnac Temple, Bt., C. B., F. B. A., F. S. A., C. I. E. Editor, "The Indian Antiquary". Rs. 6.

. . . .—*Malabar and the Dutch.* A Sequel to "Malabar and the Portuguese". By K. M. Panikkar, B. A. (Oxon.), Bar.-at-law. Rs. 6.

PANT.—*The Commercial Policy of the Moghuls.* By Dr. D. Pant, B. Com., Ph. D., Professor of Economics and History, University of Lucknow. Foreword by The Rt. Hon. Lord Meston. Rs. 6.

PHADKE.—*Sex Problems in India.* A Scientific exposition of the Sex Life and Customs prevailing in India from time immemorial. By Prof. N. S. Phadke, M. A. Foreword by Margaret Sanger. New Edition, Fully Illustrated. Rs. 6.

PICTURES *of Indian Life and Characters.* 86 reproductions depicting the people of India, their life, manners, etc. Re. 1-12.

PILLAY.—*Welfare Problems in Rural India.* By Capt. A. P. Pillay, O. B. E., M. B., B. S. With a Preface by Col. Norman Walker, and Introduction by Dr. M. I. Balfour, C. B. E. Illustrated. Rs. 8.

RAINA.—*The Co-operative Movement in India.* A Comparative Study. By J. L. Raina, B. A., M. R. A. S. (Lond.) With Foreword by P. A. Wadia, M. A. Rs. 2.

RANGA.—*Economic Organisation of Indian Villages.* By Prof. N. G. Ranga, B. Litt. (Oxon.), Dip. Econ., etc. Foreword by the Hon. V. Ramdas Pantulu, B. A., B. L., Member, Council of State, and Introduction by Dewan Bahadur A. V. Ramalinga Aiyar. Two Vols. Each Rs. 2.

. . . .—*The Economics of Handloom.* A study of the Social and Economic Conditions of Handloom Weavers of South India. By Prof. N. G. Ranga, B. Litt. (Oxon.), Dip. Econ., etc., M. L. A. Rs. 2.

RELE.—*Bhagavad Gita*. An exposition on the basis of Psycho-Philosophy and Psycho-Analysis. By Dr. V. G. Rele, F. C. P. S., L. M. & S. Rs. 4-12.

......—*The Mysterious Kundalini*. The Physical Basis of the Kundalini (Hatha) Yoga, in terms of Western Anatomy and Physiology. By Dr. V. G. Rele, F. C. P. S., L. M. & S. With a Foreword by Sir John Woodroffe. Third Revised Edition. Illustrated.

........—*The Vedic Gods as Figures of Biology*. By Dr. V. G. Rele, F. C. P. S., L. M. & S. Forewords by E. J. Thomas, M. A., D. Litt., and Y. G. Nadgir, M. S. With Ten Illustrations and a Coloured Plate. Rs. 6-8.

ROTHFIELD.—*Women of India*. By Otto Rothfield, F. R. G. S., I. C. S. (Retd.) With numerous coloured Plates, depicting Indian Women of all castes and creeds by Rao Bahadur M. V. Dhurandhar, Headmaster, Sir J. J. School of Art, Bombay. Second Edition. Rs. 11.

.........—*With Pen And Rifle In Kishtwar*. By Otto Rothfield, F. R. G. S., I. C. S. (Retd.) Illustrated. Rs. 4-8.

.......—*Umar Khayyam And His Age*. By Otto Rothfield, F. R. G. S., I. C. S. (Retd.) Rs. 7-8.

SAMADDAR.—*The Glories of Magadha*. By J. N. Samaddar. Foreword by Dr. A. Berriedale Keith. Illustrated. Rs. 8.

SHAH.—*The Splendour That Was 'Ind*. A Bird's Eye View of Indian Culture and Civilisation from the earliest times to the death of Aurangzeb. By Prof. K. T. Shah, B. Sc. Econ. (Lond.) Bar.-at-Law. With a Foreword by The Marquess of Zetland. Illustrated with Eleven Plates in colour, Three hundred and twenty-four in Half-tone and Five Maps. Rs. 30.

.....—*Sixty years of Indian Finance*. By Prof. K. T. Shah. Second Edition. Rs. 10.

......—*Federal Finance in India*. By Prof. K. T. Shah. Rs. 6.

SYED.—*Hindustani Without a Master*. A Simple Method of Learning the Hindustani or Urdu Language in three weeks. By S. B. Syed, Late Munshi, Y. M. C. A., Bombay. Re. 1-12.

TARAPOREVALA'S BOOKS ON INDIAN SUBJECTS

SYED.—*Hindustani Simplified.* By S. B. Syed, Late Munshi, Y. M. C. A., Bombay, Sixth Edition. Rs. 3-8.

TEMPLE-WRIGHT.—*Chrysanthemums: How to Grow Them.* For Amateurs in India. By Mrs. Temple-Wright. Re. 0-12.

THAKORE.—*Indian Administration to the Dawn of Responsible Government.* By B. K. Thakore, I. E. S. (Retd.) Rs. 6.

TISDALL.—*A Simplified Grammar of the Gujarati Language.* Together with a short Reading Book and Vocabulary. By The Rev. Wm. St. Clair Tisdall, M. A., C. M. S. Re. 1-8.

VAKIL.—*At Ajanta.* By Kanaiya Lal H. Vakil, B. A., LL. B. Foreword by W. E. Gladstone Solomon, I. E. S. With 88 Half-tone Illustrations. Rs. 8.

. . . .—*At Elephanta.* An illustrated handbook to the Caves of Ennery Kennery, Elephanta, Jogeshwari, and Mandapeshwar. By Kanaiya Lal H. Vakil, B. A., LL. B.

WALLACE.—*Panoramic India.* An Album of Panoramic Photographs of the beautiful monuments and natural sceneries of India. By H. R. Wallace. With a descriptive Introduction by Kanaiya Lal H. Vakil, B. A., LL. B.

YOUNG.—*Gujarati Exercises:* Or, a New mode of learning to read, write and speak the Gujarati language in six months on the Ollendorffian system. With Appendix and key for Private study. Rs. 7-8.